KARL RAHNER

KARL RAHNER

THE MYSTIC OF EVERYDAY LIFE

Harvey D. Egan, S.J.

A Crossroad Book
The Crossroad Publishing Company
New York

The Crossroad Publishing Company
370 Lexington Avenue, New York, NY 10017

Printed in the United States of America

Library of Congress Cataloging-in-Publication Data

Egan, Harvey D.
    Karl Rahner : mystic of everyday life / Harvey D. Egan.
      p.   cm. – (The Crossroad spiritual legacy series)
    Includes bibliographical references.
    ISBN 0-8245-2511-6 (pbk.)
    1. Rahner, Karl, 1904- . 2. Catholic Church – Doctrines –
History. 3. Theology – Germany – History – 20th century. I. Title.
II. Series.
BX4705.R287E37 1998
230′.2′092–dc21   97-45951
                                          CIP

1 2 3 4 5 6 7 8 9 10   02 01 00 99 98

To my Mother and Sister
and
In Memory of my Father

Contents

Preface

"Strengthened by the Church's sacraments and accompanied by the prayers of his Jesuit brothers, shortly after completing his eightieth year, Father Karl Rahner has gone home to God.... He had loved the Church and his religious Order and spent himself in their service." So reads part of the official Jesuit announcement of the death of Father Karl Rahner, S.J., on March 30, 1984. And with his death, the Church lost one of her most loyal sons.

I first met Father Rahner in 1969 when he graciously accepted the invitation to concelebrate my first Mass and to spend the day with my family and friends. Although he did not speak English (but he certainly understood it!), the fluency with which he spoke French with the French-speaking priests and parishioners of the parish impressed me. During my four years of doctoral studies under his direction, I found him to be at once utterly brilliant, shockingly creative, traditional in the best sense, original, provocative, balanced, and healing. A passion for hard work, detail, and precision and an impatience with mental laziness, theologizing for self-aggrandizement, and bureaucratic incompetence stamped his personality.

Who would not be fascinated by a theologian who loved carnivals, ice cream, large shopping malls, and being driven at very high speed — one whose olfactory curiosity cost him many dollars in New York City when a large department store demanded that he purchase all the perfume bottles he had opened? However, most impressive of all were his childlike curiosity and the simplicity, holiness, and priestliness of his Jesuit and theological life.

Perhaps the secret of Rahner's appeal is his synthesis of two elements: critical respect for the Christian tradition and unusual sensitivity to the questions and problems of contemporary life. He never doubted the Christian tradition's ability

9

to speak to the "catechism of the human heart." If revitalized, even the oldest fossils of the Christian faith could become the keys to unlock the various locks in the human person to release contemporary human authenticity. Yet, he never overlooked how difficult Christian faith is for a twentieth-century person. He could and did say to his contemporaries not only, "I am also someone who has been tempted by atheism," but also, "There is nothing more self-evident to me than God's existence."[1] Therefore, Rahner — while breathing the air of unbelief — would accept nothing less from theology than speaking about God and God's offer to us of his very own eternal life.

Impelled by his Ignatian mysticism of joy in the world — of finding God in all things and all things in God — Rahner's theology moves in two directions. He compresses all Christianity into three mysteries — Trinity, incarnation, and grace. He also unfolds these mysteries into every dimension of human life, even into a "theology of everyday things" — a theology of work, of seeing, of laughing, of eating and sleeping, and of walking and sitting. And if his theology of compression often involves anfractuous dialectics dealing with questions about the triune God, the Word made flesh, and our divinization through the Holy Spirit, his theology of unfolding can be as lovely as advising an unwed mother in her darkest hour to look into the face of her newborn for light.

Rahner not only explains critically and precisely what the Christian faith is, not only gives reasons to believe it, but he also seeks to *unite* people with it. To Rahner, theology is more than faith seeking understanding; it is as well a mystagogy that gives the people of God experiential union with this faith by leading them into their own deepest mystery. Thus, he is more a sapiential than an academic theologian.

Rahner says that "Thomas [Aquinas] was a mystic. With this I do not mean that Thomas was ever in ecstasy, or a mystic of extraordinary phenomena, or a person who in the style of the Spanish mystics was almost a bit introvertedly absorbed by his own subjective experiences. There is little or nothing about this noticeable in his writings. But he was a mystic insofar as he knew about the... *hidden* God of judging silence, about the God beyond what even the holiest theology is capable of saying about him, about the God who is loved as unfathomable — this

God he knew not only in theory but in the experience of the heart."[2]

Rahner goes on to say that "Thomas's theology is his spiritual life and his spiritual life is his theology. With him we do not yet find the horrible difference between theology and spiritual life which is often found in later theology. He thinks theologically because he needs it in his spiritual life as its most essential condition, and he thinks theologically in such a way that it can become really important for life in the concrete."[3]

What he says about St. Thomas can certainly be said of Rahner himself. I knew him as a mystic of everyday life, as a priest who constantly surrendered to God's loving incomprehensibility through a life of self-giving love, a theologian whose thinking was inseparable from his own spiritual life. When I read that St. Teresa of Avila looked for confessors and spiritual directors who were learned, humble, sympathetic to the contemplative way of life, and who possessed a "certain something" — even if they had not scaled the heights of mystical contemplation — I thought immediately of Karl Rahner. I knew him as one whose theological thinking definitely flowed from his spiritual life and whose spiritual life was nurtured by his powerful Christian thinking.

When I visited Innsbruck shortly after his death, Rahner's secretary told me that he dictated on his sick bed a long letter to the bishops of Peru supporting Gustavo Gutiérrez and his liberation theology. She also said that Rahner died without painkillers, lucid until the moment of death, like a brilliant light bulb suddenly burning out. All those with whom I spoke attested repeatedly to the awesome way in which Rahner's spirit shone forth in faith, courage, and intelligence right up to his death. I have prayed many times at his crypt beneath the Jesuit Church of the Trinity. He was always more to me than a professor. It is not without reason that I have called him the father of my theological and spiritual life. I have found myself praying not only for Rahner but *to* Rahner: "Father of my theological life and of my heart, may you be plunged more deeply into the mystery of God, be enlightened by his crucified and risen Son, and burn with the love of the Holy Spirit. Help us to live our daily humdrum lives with love and courage, to look upon the Crucified, and to be ready to die into the holy incomprehen-

sibility of God when it is our time. Meet with us daily in the
Eucharist. Amen."

For these reasons it gave me great pleasure to be asked by
the Crossroad Publishing Company to do the Karl Rahner volume for their Spiritual Legacy series. Although Rahner never
considered himself a Church Father, he definitely deserves to
be listed as one of the spiritual and theological titans in the
Christian tradition. I can only pray that the brief pages which
follow will do some justice to the enormous spiritual legacy he
has bequeathed. While writing this book I could not help mar-
veling at how powerfully Rahner speaks to the spiritual needs
of the contemporary person.

The Crossroad Publishing Company requests that the spiritual legacy volumes be approximately 60 percent quotations
from original texts. This explains the extensive use of quotations from Rahner's works throughout this book. Also, Rahner's spiritual legacy revolves around his theologically architectonic, or holistic, view of the Christian faith. Thus, I did not
shy away from trying to present his integral Christian vision;
this meant occasionally involving the reader in a few of the
more difficult aspects of his spiritual legacy. Parts of the second
chapter on St. Ignatius's influence on Rahner may prove especially challenging, but in fact one cannot read most of the great
teachers of the spiritual life without prayerful *thinking*. Finally,
because of the number of works cited in the endnotes, I felt it
unnecessary to include a bibliography of Rahner's works.

Time to complete a book is one of the most precious gifts a
person can receive. Thus I am indebted to Boston College for
this sabbatical year. I also wish to thank William V. Dych, S.J.,
and Bruce Gillette for assisting me with their expert translation
skills.

One of teaching's greatest joys is a gifted student. A few
years ago I had the honor of teaching Mary Lee Freeman, who
received her master's degree in theology from Boston College. I
am profoundly grateful for her copyediting skills, suggestions,
recommendations, and encouragement.

HARVEY D. EGAN, S.J.

Boston College, March 30, 1997
The thirteenth anniversary of Karl Rahner's death

Notes

1. *Karl Rahner in Dialogue: Conversations and Interviews, 1965–1982,* ed. Hubert Biallowons, Harvey D. Egan, S.J., and Paul Imhof, S.J. (New York: Crossroad Publishing Co., 1986), 211. Henceforth referred to as *Karl Rahner in Dialogue.*

2. "Thomas Aquinas: Monk, Theologian, and Mystic," *The Great Church Year: The Best of Karl Rahner's Homilies, Sermons, and Meditations,* ed. Albert Raffelt and Harvey D. Egan, S.J. (New York: Crossroad Publishing Co., 1993), 313. Henceforth this book will be referred to as *The Great Church Year.*

3. "Thomas Aquinas: Patron of Theological Studies," *The Great Church Year,* 316.

Chronology

March 5, 1904	Born in Freiburg in Breisgau, Germany.
1913–22	Educated at the university-oriented primary and secondary school, Realgymnasium (known today as the Kepler-Gymnasium) in Freiburg in Breisgau, Germany.
April 20, 1922	Entered the Society of Jesus at the Jesuit Novitiate of the Upper German Province in Feldkirch-Voralberg, Austria.
April 27, 1924	Pronounced First Vows of the Society of Jesus.
1924–25	Published first work, "Why We Need to Pray," *Leuchtturm* 18 (1924–25): 10–11.
1924–27	Studied philosophy at the Jesuit philosophates at Feldkirch and Pullach (near Munich).
1927–29	Spent regency years as instructor teaching Latin and other subjects at the Jesuit house of studies (juniorate) in Feldkirch-Tisis, Austria.
1929–33	Studied theology at the Jesuit theologate in Valkenburg, Holland. Published his first significant works (1932–33), focusing on Origen, Evagrius Ponticus, Bonaventure, and the history of spirituality.
July 26, 1932	Ordained priest by Michael Cardinal Faulhaber at St. Michael's Church, in Munich.
1933–34	Spent final year of Jesuit training at St. Andrea Tertianship in the Lavanttal (Carinthia), Austria.
1934–36	Undertook doctoral studies in philosophy at the University of Freiburg in Breisgau, Germany. Here he wrote *Geist im Welt: Zur Metaphysik der endlichen Erkenntnis bei Thomas von Aquin.*

December 19, 1936 Received doctorate in theology from the University of Innsbruck. Wrote the dissertation entitled "The Origin of the Church as Second Eve from the Side of Christ the Second Adam: An Investigation of the Typological Significance of John 19:34."

July 1, 1937 Completed the postdoctoral work (*Habilitation*) required for university teaching. Appointed lecturer in dogmatic theology at the University of Innsbruck.

1938 Published the first edition of *Worte in Schweigen* (ET: *Encounters with Silence*).

August 15, 1939 Pronounced solemn vows at St. Andrea Tertianship in the Lavanttal, Carinthia.

October 1939 Nazis abolished the theology faculty at the University of Innsbruck. Rahner banished from the region by a "district prohibition" (*Gauverbot*).

1939 Published the first edition of *Geist im Welt: Zur Metaphysik der endlichen Erkenntnis bei Thomas von Aquin* (ET: *Spirit in the World*) and *Aszese und Mystik in der Väterzeit* (a revision of the 1933 French work of M. Viller).

1939–44 Appointed university lecturer in Vienna. Became a colleague of Cardinal Innitzer's diocesan staff at the Pastoral Institute in Vienna. Began lecture circuit.

1941 Published the first edition of *Hörer des Wortes: Zur Grundlegung einer Religionsphilosophie* (ET: *Hearer of the Word: Laying the Foundation for a Philosophy of Religion*).

1944–45 Served as parish priest in Mariakirchen, Bavaria, from July 1944 to August 1945.

1945–48 Worked as professor of dogmatic theology at the Jesuit theologate in Pullach, near Munich. Also taught theology courses in priestly formation at the Munich Educational Center.

August 1948 Returned to the theology faculty at the University of Innsbruck.

June 30, 1949 — Promoted to Ordinary Professor of Dogma and the History of Dogma at the University of Innsbruck. Published the first edition of *Von der Not und dem Segen des Gebetes* (ET: *On the Need and the Blessing of Prayer*).

March 31, 1954 — Accepted invitation to join Associé de la Société Philosophique de Louvain, Belgium.

1954 — Published *Kleines Kirchenjahr* (ET: *The Eternal Year*); first volume of *Schriften zur Theologie* (ET: *Theological Investigations I*).

1957–68 — Coedited, with Josef Höfer, the second edition of the thirteen-volume *Lexikon für Theologie und Kirche,* the last three being commentaries on the documents of the Second Vatican Council.

1958–84 — Coedited (until 1978 with Heinrich Schlier) the 101-volume *Quaestiones Disputatae.*

1959 — Published the first edition of pastoral theology essays, entitled *Sendung und Gnade* (Three-volume ET: *The Christian Commitment; Theology for Renewal;* and *The Christian in the Market Place*).

1961 — Named by Pope John XXIII as advisor to Cardinal Königs to prepare for the Second Vatican Council. Coauthored, with Herbert Vorgrimler, the first edition of *Kleines Theologisches Wörterbuch* (ET: *Dictionary of Theology*).

1962–63 — Object of a special censorship from the "Holy Office."

1962 — Named an official *peritus* (expert) for the Second Vatican Council by Pope John XXIII.

1964–69 — Coedited with many others the five-volume *Handbuch der Pastoraltheologie.*

January 20, 1964 — Received a medal of honor bestowed by the Tirolean government in recognition of his academic achievements.

March 5, 1964 — Appointed University Professor of Christian Weltanschauung and the Philosophy of Religion at the University of Munich, as the successor of Romano Guardini.

May 13, 1964	Awarded Doctor of Theology, honoris causa, by the University of Münster in Westfalen — the first of fifteen honorary doctorates.
June 26, 1965	Received the Reuchlin Prize from the city of Pforzheim.
1967–69	Coedited with Adolf Darlap the four-volume *Sacramentum Mundi: An Encyclopedia of Theology.*
April 1, 1967	Appointed University Professor of Dogma and the History of Dogma on the faculty of Catholic Theology at the University of Münster in Westfalen.
1968–74	Coedited with Herbert Vorgrimler the *Internationale Dialog Zeitschrift.*
April 1, 1968	Received the University of Helsinki Medal in Finland.
April 27, 1969	Became a member of the papal International Theological Commission, from which he freely resigned in 1971.
1970–75	Served as a member of the Synod of German Bishops.
March 18, 1970	Received the Romano Guardini Prize from the Catholic Academy in Bavaria (Munich).
May 6, 1970	Received West Germany's Distinguished Cross of Merit with Star.
June 23, 1970	Inducted into the German Order of Merit for Arts and Sciences.
September 3, 1971	Became professor emeritus at the University of Münster in Westfalen.
October 1, 1971	Appointed Honorary Professor of Interdisciplinary Questions Relating to Philosophy and Theology at the Jesuit philosophate in Munich.
May 10, 1972	Inducted in Boston as an honorary member of the American Academy of Arts and Sciences.
June 18, 1972	Appointed Honorary Professor of Dogma and the History of Dogma in the Department of Catholic Theology at the University of Innsbruck.

1972	Published *Strukturwandel der Kirche* (ET: *The Shape of the Church to Come*).
October 20, 1973	Received the 1973 Sigmund Freud Prize for Scholarly Prose from the German Academy for Language and Literature.
July 10, 1974	Inducted as a Corresponding Fellow of the British Academy.
July 15, 1974	Received the Lorenz Werthmann Medal from West Germany's Caritas Society.
November 6, 1974	Received the Campion Award of the Catholic Book Club of America Press.
1976	Published the first edition of *Grundkurs des Glaubens: Einführung in den Begriff des Christentums* (ET: *Foundations of Christian Faith: An Introduction to the Idea of Christianity*).
September 4, 1976	Received the 1976 Cardinal Innitzer Prize.
1978	Published *Ignatius von Loyola*, with P. Imhof and H. N. Loose.
March 1, 1979	Appointed Honorary Member of the Commonwealth of Kentucky, in Frankfort, Kentucky.
March 27, 1979	Received the Père Marquette Discovery Award from the University of Marquette in Milwaukee.
April 1, 1979	Appointed Honorary Member of Alpha Sigma Nu, the National Jesuit Honor Society.
April 3, 1979	Awarded keys to the city of Louisville, Kentucky. Also made a "Colonel" of Kentucky.
May 16, 1979	Received Cultural Prize of Honor from the city of Munich.
October 1981	Returned to live and work at the Jesuit University in Innsbruck.
1984	Published the sixteenth volume of *Schriften zur Theologie* (ET: *Theological Investigations XXII and XXIII*).
March 30, 1984	Died in Innsbruck.

Chapter 1

A Rahner Biography

Karl Rahner has been aptly called "the quiet mover of the Roman Catholic Church" and the "Father of the Catholic Church in the twentieth century." His four thousand written works indicate that he wrote on all significant theological topics, on sensitive ecclesiological questions, and even on devotional practices. A great ecumenist, he entered into dialogue with atheist, Buddhist, Jewish, Marxist, Muslim, Protestant, and scientific thinkers the world over. He may well be the theological titan of the twentieth century. Yet Rahner referred to himself as someone who was "not particularly industrious," who "went to bed early," and who was a "poor sinner." "All I want to be," he said, "even in this work [of theology], is a human being, a Christian, and, as well as I can, a priest of the Church."[1]

Early Years

Rahner was born in Germany in the city of Freiburg in Breisgau on March 5, 1904, one of seven children in what he described as a "perfectly normal Christian family."[2] His father was a respected gymnasium professor whom Rahner spoke of as "thoroughly Christian";[3] his mother, who lived to the age of 101, was a "very religious" and "very courageous" yet dreadfully scrupulous woman whose sense of responsibility impelled her to assume duties she might just as easily have dropped.[4] Later Rahner was to recall with marked affection that his mother nervously followed his career, fearful that he would become proud.

Rahner said that when he was growing up, there was always enough to eat. However, in order to support the family his father had to tutor on the side and his mother to baby-sit to bring in extra money. Yet all the children attended university-oriented secondary schools, obtained their diplomas, and went on for university studies.

Rahner attended primary and secondary school in Freiburg, considered himself an average student, and found his lessons somewhat boring. From his school days he remembered boys and girls together in the same class, as were Jews, Protestants, and Catholics; the atmosphere was tolerant, liberal, and humanitarian, as things in Freiburg generally were. Rahner suspected that he stood out somewhat from his classmates because of a marked religious sense, for example, his frequent reading of the fourth book of the *Imitation of Christ*, frequent Communion, and his own short thanksgivings after Mass. Along with his oldest sister and friends, he translated Latin hymns by Thomas Aquinas into German.[5] Despite these peculiarities, Rahner seemed to be liked by his classmates and was chosen as class representative.

A temperance youth movement called *Quickborn* ("Fountain of Youth") seemed to have been important to the young Rahner. "It was more a grass-roots than a church-directed affair. But it was still Catholic, religious, extremely active and intense. There too I was influenced positively in many ways that affected my future life, especially since that was when I first met Romano Guardini at Castle Rothenfels."[6]

Jesuit Formation

On April 22, 1922, Rahner entered the novitiate of the Upper German Province of the Society of Jesus, which at that time was in Feldkirch in Voralberg, Austria. Although he was following in the footsteps of his brother Hugo, who had entered three years prior, Rahner did not seem to be influenced by his brother's decision. It seemed to amuse Rahner in later life that his parents "had the impression that [he] wasn't suited for the Jesuits because [he] was too gruff and too unsocial."[7] Even his "very intelligent" if somewhat dry religion teacher was skeptical: "No, Karl isn't suited for that. He's too withdrawn and grumpy."[8] Rahner's reaction to this: "Well, by God, it happened all the same, and has lasted for sixty years. But it does show that this thoroughly Christian family atmosphere was still not of the sort to shape a person by hook or by crook in a narrowly clerical way."[9]

In the novitiate Rahner devoted himself wholly to the spiritual life and to intense study of Jesuit spirituality and the great spiritual writers. As a novice he wrote his first article for the journal *Leuchtturm* ("Lighthouse") on a topic to which he often returned, "Why We Need to Pray."

After completing two years of novitiate and taking his Jesuit vows, Rahner began the normal course of studies for Jesuits at that time. In 1924–25, he spent his first year studying philosophy at Feldkirch; his second and third years of philosophical studies were in Pullach near Munich. Here he was introduced both to Catholic scholastic philosophy and to the great German modern philosophers. His many notebooks indicate clearly the intensity with which he studied Kant and two contemporary Thomists, the Belgian Jesuit Joseph Maréchal (1878–1944) and the French Jesuit Pierre Rousselot (1878–1915). These two Jesuits profoundly influenced the way Rahner was later to interpret St. Thomas Aquinas. In fact Rahner attributed to Maréchal his "initial, truly philosophical insight."[10] Not only did Maréchal attempt to make Kant's transcendental method fruitful for Thomistic epistemology, but he was also concerned with questions of mysticism and mystical experience, especially how the contemporary person could experience God. These themes are at the heart of Rahner's theology.

Jesuit training normally includes a period of practical work between the study of philosophy and theology, the so-called regency period. During this time from 1927 to 1929, Rahner was assigned to teach Latin to the novices at Feldkirch. His mastery of Latin was not only to give him access later on to the Western philosophical and theological tradition, but also would enable him to communicate fluently with non-German speakers at the Second Vatican Council and on many other occasions. In fact, the first time I heard Rahner speak was at the Jesuit School of Philosophy and Theology in Weston, Massachusetts, in 1964 when he addressed the faculty and seminarians in fluent Latin.

One of Rahner's novice students of Latin was Alfred Delp, who later became one of the conspirators of the Kreisauer circle against Hitler. Arrested by the Nazis on July 28, 1944, he pronounced his final Jesuit vows handcuffed and was hanged in

Berlin on February 2, 1945. Rahner would later recall his friendship with Delp, whom he considered to be in "the front ranks of those witnesses who were motivated by Christianity to resist the evils of Nazism."[11]

In 1929 Rahner began his theological studies at the Jesuit theologate in Valkenburg, Holland. Although superiors had indicated that at the end of his training he would teach the history of philosophy, Rahner never regarded theology as being in any way secondary. In fact, he stated emphatically that during his studies in Valkenburg he was already "interested in theological questions, above all in spiritual theology, in the history of piety, in patristic mysticism, and also in Bonaventure."[12] And here he mastered large areas of patristic theology, a proficiency evinced throughout his life. His first serious publications (1932–34) on the notion of the spiritual senses in Origen and Bonaventure and his 1939 book *Aszese und Mystik in der Väterzeit* bear witness to his intense research in the Christian spiritual-mystical tradition. Of special importance in this regard was the collaboration with his brother Hugo on both patristics and the spirituality of St. Ignatius of Loyola — the latter indelibly stamping Rahner's theology of grace, repentance, prayer, discernment of spirits, and existential ethics.

On July 26, 1932, Rahner was ordained priest and then undertook the one remaining year of required theological study. Tertianship, the final year of Jesuit preparation, is devoted to prayer and to gaining pastoral experience before starting one's formal ministry. This Rahner completed at St. Andrea, the Jesuit tertianship in Austria.

Advanced Studies

Because Rahner's superiors had decided that he was to teach the history of philosophy at Pullach, he returned to his home town of Freiburg in 1934 to study for the doctorate in philosophy. Because of Heidegger's Nazi leanings, Rahner selected instead Martin Honecker as his dissertation director, but he attended seminars taught by Heidegger — the only professor he ever called a great master. Honecker eventually rejected the dissertation, a creative interpretation of Aquinas's epistemology influenced by the transcendental Thomism of Joseph Maréchal.

The rejected dissertation is the now famous book *Spirit in the World*, published in 1939 and translated into many languages. Because Rahner had already been reassigned to teach theology in Innsbruck, the failure meant nothing. In fact, Rahner said: "To be frank, I myself had no great inner attraction to the history of philosophy. Certainly I would have been a quite respectable historian of philosophy, but my heart didn't bleed when I was reassigned by my superiors."[13]

He completed his doctoral studies in theology without incident. Returning to a topic that had long interested him — the typological interpretation of John 19:34, a theme dear to some Church Fathers — Rahner quickly finished his dissertation, entitled, "The Origin of the Church as Second Eve from the Side of Christ the Second Adam: An Investigation of the Typological Significance of John 19:34." Of this dissertation he said: "I had also written a small, lousy, but at least, according to the standards of the time, adequate theological dissertation."[14]

The War Years

On route to his new post to teach theology in Innsbruck, Rahner delivered a series of fifteen lectures in Salzburg — eventually published in 1941 as *Hearer of the Word*, his second foundational work. The beginning of the winter term at Innsbruck in 1937 was for Rahner the start of his thirty-four-year career as professor of theology. However, only a year after his arrival, the Nazis took over the university and essentially banished Rahner to Vienna. There, as a member of the diocesan Pastoral Institute, he spent most of the war years — the final year as a parish priest in the Bavarian village of Mariakirchen. In Munich in 1946, he preached his now famous Lenten sermons, later published under the title *The Need and the Blessing of Prayer.*

In so many ways, Rahner's theology is supremely pastoral. Perhaps his priestly work in war-ravaged Europe during and after the Second World War further developed his already spontaneous inclination toward the pastoral care of individuals and the concerns of a Church in "diaspora." In fact, many of his writings are essays prepared for particular occasions or in response to questions as they arose — not the overly systematic and encyclopedic approach considered typical of German theologians of his age. Rahner's pastoral side shows itself in yet another significant way: his theology often begins and ends in prayer. In fact, explicit prayers and penetrating reflection on prayer punctuate his entire theological life, as his widely read *Encounters with Silence* and *Prayers for a Lifetime* illustrate. Thus, Rahner stands in a long line of great Christian theologians who were likewise great teachers of prayer.

Professor, Writer, Preacher

In 1948 Rahner began to teach in the reconstituted theology faculty at Innsbruck and began his incredibly prolific period of writing, lecturing, and publishing. It is somewhat ironic that he was not able to find a Catholic publisher in Germany interested in what was to be one of the theological wonders of the twentieth century: the monumental sixteen-volume (twenty-three in English) *Theological Investigations*. The Swiss publisher Benziger finally agreed, and the first three volumes were published in 1954–56.

Rahner also edited the twenty-eighth to the thirty-first editions of Denziger's *Enchiridion Symbolorum,* coedited the thirteen-volume *Lexikon für Theologie und Kirche* (1957–68), the 101-volume (at his death) *Quaestiones Disputatae* (1958–84), the four-volume *Sacramentum Mundi* (1967–69), the five volume *Handbuch der Pastoraltheologie* (1964–69), the five-volume compendium of dogmatic theology *Mysterium Salutis* (1965–76), and the thirty-volume encyclopedia *Christian Faith in Modern Society* (1980–83). He founded the international theological journal *Concilium* in 1965 and coedited with Herbert Vorgrimler the international journal *Dialog* (1968–74). He also contributed many articles and volumes to these works. During his 1961 summer vacation Rahner and Vorgrimler wrote the immensely popular *Dictionary of Theology.*

Rahner never ceased his pastoral activities during this period. In 1959 he published twenty-four articles on a variety of pastoral themes, translated in English in three volumes as *The Christian Commitment, Theology for Renewal,* and *The Christian in the Market Place.* His letters to young people in the volume entitled *Is Christian Life Possible Today?* evince his personal style of spiritual direction, while both *The Priesthood* and *Spiritual Exercises* demonstrate his prowess as a retreat director. *The Great Church Year,* a collection of his sermons and homilies, shows why Rahner ranks in the tradition of Christian theologians who were also great preachers.

It says much about Rahner that he did not accept invitations to lecture based upon the size, level, or social importance of his audience. He spoke to university audiences throughout the world, study groups, retreat directors, superiors of religious Orders, university chaplains, journalists, associations for wives and mothers, devotional associations, pastoral congresses, family and education groups, philosophical societies, student groups, sociologists, and the like. I witnessed him agreeing to speak to a women's informal prayer group, despite his exhausting schedule, because they told him this was important "for the salvation of their souls."

Moreover, Rahner had an uncanny ability when it came to finding money, food, clothing, and shelter for the needy and downtrodden who sought him out. He possessed the knack, too, of shanghaiing others into assisting him with his practical works of charity. One of the things I remember most vividly is how we two went grocery shopping in a large supermarket and drove two hours to take the food to a widow and to find her a place to live. One of Rahner's last public acts after the celebration of his eightieth birthday was to appeal for funds to purchase a motorbike for a missionary in Africa.

The countless ways in which he brought meaning, comfort, light, relief, and healing to so many persons prompted one distinguished German author to call Rahner "a most effective psychotherapist." For example, I know how priestly and generous with his time Rahner was to a young Jesuit friend who was leaving the priesthood. Students who understood very little of his lectures told me that they attended because they "felt better" about themselves in his presence. "This is a professor to whom I can confess," one said. Not many years before his death, Rahner often spent several hours of his intensely busy day helping a young German psychiatrist to recover some of the memory he had lost in a serious auto accident.

One of the most absurd statements I ever read about Rahner's theology was that there is nothing priestly, kerygmatic, or pastoral about it. It can and should be said of him that his theology is supremely pastoral and that its major focus is "Salus animarum suprema lex" (The salvation of souls is the supreme law).

Difficulties with Rome — due mainly to Rahner's views on eucharistic issues and Mariology — came to a head in 1962. A short-lived special censorship ended in May 1963 — several months after he had been appointed one of the official *periti*, or theological experts, of the Second Vatican Council (1962–65), a council whose theological outlook he influenced decisively. During this period, he also became the successor to Romano Guardini in the Chair of Christian Weltanschauung at the University of Munich on March 5, 1964.

Because Rahner was and desired to remain a theologian and many of his students went to Munich to study *theology*, he soon found his situation there unusual. His chair was in the philosophical faculty, and he was not allowed to prepare students for the degree in theology. Thus, when he received an invitation to teach at the University of Münster, he replied (with the approval of the minister of education at the time and of Cardinal Döpfner): "I'll stay in Munich if I'm allowed to have doctoral students." As he later explained, "That was because I wanted an assistant and co-workers who would receive doctorates in theology.... For all practical purposes the theology faculty refused me this rather harmless and in other respects obvious and reasonable request. Then the only thing I could really say was: 'Good, then I'll accept the appointment to Münster.' Guardini was very disappointed in me and vexed about this. Still, there was nothing I could do."[15]

Thus, on April 1, 1967, he was appointed to what was to be his final teaching position as professor of dogmatic theology in Münster, where he taught from 1967 until his retirement in 1971. One of the courses he gave over two semesters both at Munich and Münster was subsequently published under the title *Foundations of Christian Faith: An Introduction to the Idea of Christianity*. Translated into many languages, this highly acclaimed book may be the closest thing to a systematic, architectonic summary of his theology.

Living at the Jesuit writers' house in Munich from 1971 to 1981 and afterward in Innsbruck, Rahner continued his unrelenting worldwide lecturing, writing, and pastoral activity. Seeming retrenchment on Church reform, unfair criticism of the official Church, and the loss of ecumenical zeal — among other things — concerned him at this time. He and Heinrich Fries wrote the groundbreaking book *Unity of the Churches: An Actual Possibility* in 1983. Becoming ill a few days after the celebrations of his eightieth birthday, he died on March 30, 1984.

Notes

1. "Selbstporträt," *Forscher und Gelehrte*, ed. W. Ernst Böhm (Stuttgart: Battenberg, 1966), 21. For the best biographical sketch of Karl Rahner to date, see Herbert Vorgrimler, *Understanding Karl Rahner: An Introduction to His Life and Thought* (New York: Crossroad Publishing Co., 1986). For further autobiographical information, see *Karl Rahner — I Remember: An Autobiographical Interview with Meinold Krauss*, trans. and intro. Harvey D. Egan, S.J. (New York: Crossroad Publishing Co., 1985). Henceforth referred to as *Karl Rahner — I Remember*.

2. *Karl Rahner — I Remember*, 24.

3. *Karl Rahner in Dialogue*, 337.

4. *Bekenntnisse*, ed. Georg Sporschill, S.J. (Munich: Herold Verlag, 1984), 20.

5. Ibid., 15–16.

6. *Karl Rahner — I Remember*, 28.

7. *Faith in a Wintry Season: Interviews and Conversations with Karl Rahner in the Last Years of His Life, 1982–84*, ed. Hubert Biallowons, Harvey D. Egan, S.J., and Paul Imhof, S.J. (New York: Crossroad Publishing Co., 1990), 95. Henceforth referred to as *Faith in a Wintry Season*.

8. *Karl Rahner — I Remember*, 26.

9. Ibid.

10. *Karl Rahner in Dialogue*, 14.

11. *Karl Rahner — I Remember*, 39–40.

12. *Faith in a Wintry Season*, 16.

13. Ibid., 44.

14. Ibid., 16.

15. *Karl Rahner — I Remember*, 75.

Chapter 2

Karl Rahner —
Ignatian Theologian

Commentators have emphasized correctly the intellectual influence of Thomas Aquinas, Bonaventure, Maréchal, Heidegger, Hegel, and Kant upon Karl Rahner. However, most miss the secret of his extraordinarily profound and attractive theology: the significant role played therein by the spirituality of St. Ignatius of Loyola and his *Spiritual Exercises*,[1] a masterpiece of meditations and contemplations on Christ's life, death, and resurrection. Rahner himself says that the Ignatian spirituality he assimilated through prayer and his Jesuit formation is more significant and important for him than all the philosophy and theology he learned both inside and outside the Society of Jesus.[2] He admits that even his decision to enter the Jesuit Order was not absolutely momentous for him until he experienced deeply its Ignatian spirituality.[3] Two thirty-day retreats and yearly eight-day retreats based on the Ignatian *Exercises* were part of Rahner's sixty-two Jesuit years. From the time of his ordination in 1932 until his death in 1984, Rahner gave and preached on these Exercises over fifty times. His books entitled *Spiritual Exercises*[4] and *The Priesthood*[5] — to name only two works — attest to his expertise as a director and preacher of Ignatian retreats.

The meditations and contemplations of the *Exercises* are organized into four "weeks." This designation is based not on seven chronological days, but upon the specific graces sought and granted as a result of each week's exercises. In fact, "the time should be set according to the needs of the subject matter" (*Exercises*, no. 4). The first week corresponds to the purgative way (*Exercises*, no. 10); the second week, to the illuminative way (*Exercises,* no. 10); the third and fourth weeks, to the unitive way. The latter two weeks also deepen — in the light of Christ's passion and resurrection — the "election," the decision concerning one's state or reform of life made at the end of the second week.

The *Spiritual Exercises* contain not only the fruits of Ignatius's personal mysticism and spirituality, but also of his pastoral experience. They can be called the school of prayer created for and taught by the Society of Jesus. Ignatius composed them as a manual for the person giving them (the retreat director). They are to be experienced — not read or studied — by the one making them (the exercitant).

The *Exercises* initiate a dialogue between the exercitant and the retreat director; between the exercitant, the director, and the text itself; between the exercitant and the "true essentials" of the Christian faith; between the exercitant and God, who will work directly with him or her; and between the exercitant and the "signs of the times."

When asked on his eightieth birthday what he wished to bequeath as his last will and testament, Rahner pointed unhesitatingly to the essay "Ignatius of Loyola Speaks to a Modern Jesuit."[6] In this spiritual gem, Rahner put himself in Ignatius's place to speak to contemporary Jesuits. Not only did he call this masterpiece his last will and testament, but he also considered it a résumé of his theology in general and of how he tried to live.[7] Only a few months before he died, when asked by an interviewer what question he asked himself, Rahner replied: "What can I hope for? I can only say, for God's light, eternity, and mercy. And I hope to be able to pray along with Teresa of Avila: 'Let nothing disturb you...God alone suffices,' and with Ignatius of Loyola, 'Take, Lord, and receive...give me your love and your grace; that is enough for me.' Both these prayers are more than just words; they embody a whole way of life."[8] In essence they mean that "God loves me and I can love him. I love him because he has given me the power to love him and therein I have finally lost myself in God."[9]

The Ignatian prayer which Rahner mentions concludes the *Exercises.* The full prayer is: "Take, Lord, and receive all my liberty, my memory, my understanding, and all my will — all that I have and possess. You, Lord, have given all that to me. I now give it back to you, O Lord. All of it is yours. Dispose of it according to your will. Give me love of yourself along with your grace, for that is enough for me" (no. 234). Rahner says that in this prayer Ignatius puts himself completely and without reserve into God's hands and that he "ranks *freedom* ahead of the Augustinian trinity (memory, understanding, will). I do not believe," Rahner continues, "this was only a chance selection of words and rhetoric. I also do not believe that traditional Jesuit theology has taken this seriously enough. I also do not know if I have really done better by it in my theology, but still I did try somewhat."[10]

The following poetic description Rahner gives of Ignatius speaks for itself: "Ignatius has something almost of the archaic and archetypal about him. That explains what at a first superficial glance one might call the medieval features of his spiritual character. He has nothing that really belongs to the Baroque or the Renaissance about him. The features that are held to justify interpretation in those terms, his individualism, deliberate reflection, his almost technically regulated self-mastery, his silence and discretion, his subordination of the highly self-aware person to the objective task, the slight skepticism which pervades everything though without lyrical self-expression or self-conscious melancholy, these and similar traits are not really 'Baroque' and 'modern,' even if in other connections the distinguishing mark of the 'Baroque' and of 'modernity' is the individual's awareness of himself as individual, exulting in himself or intoxicated with his own problems and complexity, a self-mirroring individuality. None of that is to be observed in Ignatius."[11]

However, Rahner does consider St. Ignatius of Loyola one of the central figures in the development of spirituality at the start of modernity, which focuses on the rational, the planned, the scientific, and the technical.[12] Because of Ignatius's emphasis upon the subject, interiority, the subjective striving for self-reflection, self-responsibility, and salvation, Rahner views him as *the* modern par excellence.[13]

And of the *Exercises* penned by Ignatius, Rahner maintains that they "are a fundamental document of the post-Reformation Church, which had a decisive influence upon its history.... The *Exercises* brought something genuinely new into the Church which in the present situation of 'the end of modernity' is both passing away and being maintained in a remarkable way."[14]

Rahner deems Ignatius's *Exercises* to be inspired by the Holy Spirit and underscores their fundamental, archetypal, and even prophetic quality. Just as theologians turn to Scripture and to the Church's Tradition as theological sources, Rahner insists they should do likewise with Ignatius's creative type of spiritual literature.[15] Rahner assesses the *Exercises* as a "literature of piety which forestalls theological reflection, which is more fundamentally spontaneous than the latter, wiser and more experienced than the wisdom of the learned.... This is a spiritual literature which is ... a 'creative,' original assimilation of God's revelation in Christ. It occurs as a creative prototype in accord with historical circumstances, ... as a new gift by God's Spirit of primitive Christianity to a new age.... If this is correct, the Exercises can form a subject of tomorrow's theology."[16]

Because of his conviction that the *Exercises* can and should set the task for future theology, he frequently laments that their philosophical and theological riches for the most part remain unexplored.[17] "One has the impression," Rahner writes, "that Jesuits have regarded Ignatius as a pious and holy man whose achievements earned him an important place in the Church's history. But he has scarcely been treated in his own right as one of the central figures in the development of spirituality at the beginning of modernity. Thus Jesuits have a duty toward the founder of the Order which has not yet been fulfilled in their theological work. To the retort that Ignatius was no theologian, one should point out that he was more, not less, than a theologian, and in consequence can set tasks even for tomorrow's theology."[18]

Unlike some theologians who look condescendingly on "pious" literature, Rahner was stimulated to work out the theological implications contained in the *Spiritual Exercises* of St. Ignatius of Loyola.[19] "[My] own theological thinking," he declares, "sprang from the practice of the Ignatian Exercises and so in fact was fashioned in the light of reflection on the effective operation of the Spirit."[20] Shortly before his death Rahner said somewhat proudly: "I hope that the great founder of my religious Order will concede that in my theology a little bit from his spirit and from his own spirituality is perceptible. At least I hope it is! I am even of the immodest opinion that in this or that point I stand closer to Ignatius than the great Jesuit theology of the Baroque period which did not always do justice, and this in not insignificant points, to Ignatius's legitimate existentialism, if I may put it that way."[21]

Thus, in a variety of ways Rahner looks to St. Ignatius as the first existentialist. That Ignatius mentions *freedom* before memory, understanding, and will in his "Take and Receive" prayer — as mentioned above — deeply impressed Rahner. Thus, reflection upon the theological implications of the Ignatian *Exercises* may account for Rahner's shift from an emphasis upon knowledge in his early writings to one upon freedom in his later works.

Rahner understands the human person as a self-conscious and free being, as one endowed with the capability to co-create oneself freely with God the way one will *be* for all eternity. Eternity is born through freedom exercised in time. In short, persons actually become their free decisions. Thus freedom is not the ability to do this or that; rather, it is the ability to say yes or no to God with one's entire being.

The Experience of God

The Ignatian Exercises — especially numbers 15 and 16 — imparted to Rahner one of the main pillars of his theological thought: God's experiential self-communication. Ignatius was convinced that during the Exercises the exercitant experiences the *immediacy* of God's self-communication and that the Creator and the creature work directly with each other. This Ignatian insight is almost a short formula for the entire Rahnerian enterprise. His theological point of departure is nothing less than a genuine, original experience of God, a starting point he himself experienced. For Rahner, theology must "point to that quite specific experience to which St. Ignatius wished to guide and direct spiritual practice through his Exercises."[22] When asked just a few years before his death what he considered the most important contemporary problems, he said without hesitation: "The oldest ones, which are in fact always the most relevant: How is an authentic experience of God possible? How can I truly experience that in Jesus Christ God has communicated himself to us in an absolute and irreversible way?"[23]

The words which Rahner put into the mouth of St. Ignatius of Loyola in his last will and testament speak eloquently about Rahner's own priestly, theological life. They reveal Rahner's soul and his vocation. "You know that I wanted 'to help souls'...therefore to say something about God, his grace, and about Jesus Christ, the crucified and risen one, so that their freedom would be redeemed in God's freedom. I wished to say this in the same way the Church has always said it, and still I think, with good reason, that I could say the old freshly. Why? I was convinced that...I experienced God directly and I wish to communicate this experience to others, as well as I can. If I thus claim to have had a direct experience of God...I mean only that I experienced God, the ineffable and unfathomable one, the silent yet near one, in his trinitarian bestowal upon me. I experienced God also and especially beyond all images— who when he thus approaches in his grace cannot be confused in any way with anything else....I have experienced God himself, not human words about him....This experience is truly grace, but for that reason it is nonetheless essentially refused to no one. Of that I am convinced....One thing remains certain: God can and will deal directly with his creature. That *this* happens, a person can truly experience. He can grasp the sovereign disposition of God's freedom over his life, which can no longer be figured out by the noisy human arguments from earthly wisdom—neither philosophically nor theologically nor existentially....One thing remains certain: a person can experience God's very own self."[24] I consider this to be the most precious gift Rahner bestows to us from his spiritual legacy.

According to him, God's self-communication, grace, is at the heart of human existence. To be human is to be graced, the recipient of God's offer of self. To one commentator's observation that Rahner's theology of grace derives from the traditional theology of the schools, Rahner rejoined: "[My theology of grace] is based on much earlier attempts at a theological consideration of the *experience of grace*, which *Ignatian spirituality* is particularly aware of....The experience of grace is continually shared by every Christian in the forgiving encounter with God in the act of repentance."[25] In fact, Rahner never accepted the traditional

Jesuit theology of grace because he contended that we *con-sciously* experience grace, that is, the working of the divinizing Spirit of God within us.

To Rahner, the experience of God ineradicably rooted in the depths of the human being constitutes human dignity. A person must deal with the depths of his or her being, with the ultimate mystery of life. When an interviewer said to Rahner: "I have never had an experience of God," Rahner quickly retorted: "I don't believe you; I just don't accept that. You have had, perhaps, no experience of God under this precise label *God* but you have had or have now an experience of God — and I am convinced that this is true of every person.... This inner experience of God is naturally and necessarily very difficult to describe. What love is, what fidelity is, what longing is, what immediate responsibility is — are all things that are difficult to reflect upon and to express. We begin to stutter, and what we say sounds very strange, laborious, and clumsy. But that is no proof that a person has not experienced fidelity, responsibility, joy, true love, and so on. So it is with the experience of God."[26] Thus, Rahner concedes only that people often misunderstand him because they use different words to express what are nonetheless experiences of God.

Moreover, Rahner adds, "this experience of God should not be discredited as a mere mood carrying no conviction, or as an unverifiable feeling. Nor is it merely a factor in our private interior lives. On the contrary it has a fully social and public significance.... It is of course different from that conceptual knowledge of individual things *within* the sphere of knowledge. In fact it bears upon the totality of knowledge and freedom as such....

"For it is present irremovably, however unacknowledged and unreflected upon it may be, in every exercise of the spiritual faculties even at the most rational level by virtue of the fact that every such exercise draws its life from the prior apprehension of the all-transcending whole which is the mystery, one and nameless. It is possible to suppress this experience, but it remains, and at the decisive moments of our lives it breaks in upon our awareness once more with irresistible force. Nor can we say that we should be silent about it on the grounds that we cannot speak 'clearly' about it....

"And if the rationalist philosophers and positivists are unwilling to speak about it, does this mean that the saints, the poets, and other revealers of the fullness of existence as a *whole* must also be forbidden to speak? The word 'God' is there, and it asserts itself even in the struggle which the atheist wages against it. And will this term 'God' not raise the question ever anew of what is meant by it? And even if this term were ever to be forgotten, even then in the decisive moments of our lives we should still constantly, though silently, be encompassed by this nameless mystery of our existence, judging us and endowing us with the grace of our ultimate freedom, and we would discover the ancient name for it anew."[27] In short, the experience of God is not only ineradicably present in the human heart but it also possesses social significance. It is thus the very ground of all conceptual knowledge and rationality.

The Experience of the Triune God

Ignatius had experienced mystically not only "God" and the "Trinity" but also the Father *as Father,* the Son *as Son,* and the Holy Spirit *as Holy Spirit.* Ignatius's trinitarian mysticism influenced Rahner's emphasis upon the *trinitarian* dimension of grace and his bold statement that the "economic" Trinity (the Trinity of salvation history) is the "immanent" Trinity (the eternal Trinity), and vice versa.[28] This means that God gives *himself* to us as Father, as Son, and as Holy Spirit — and nothing less. From the way that God gives himself to us in salvation history, we know that the eternal God is in fact triune self-giving.

Rahner views the human person as someone intrinsically and experientially related to the ever-greater God (Father) who has appeared in history (Son) and who loves us in the core of our being (Holy Spirit). God graces the person with nothing less than himself as mystery, revelation, and love.[29] The triune God who communicates his very own self to us — not an abstract God — stands at the center of Rahner's theology. Whether or not we are explicitly conscious of it, whether or not we open ourselves to it, our whole being is directed toward a holy, loving Mystery who is the basis of our existence. Even prior to baptism, either by water or by desire, every person is already redeemed, subject to this self-communicating God's universal salvific will, and obliged to live for his or her supernatural destiny.

The God of mystery, revelation, and love offers *self* to everyone with a certain immediacy to share his own divine life. For Rahner, therefore, there is no such thing as the "natural" person, because all creation is graced with the offer of God's self-communication even prior to any human response. This means that there was never a time or a place in which God did not offer himself to all persons. Hence, everyone must say yes or no to God's self-offer freely with one's entire being.[30]

In Rahner's view, God's self-offer as mystery, revelation, and love actually constitutes human identity. To be human in its most radical sense means to be the addressee of God's offer of self. Expressed differently, the human person is a mysterious, total question. Only the incomprehensible God can and has fully answered this question in his enfleshed Word. In every human heart, a divine-human drama is taking place — the drama of God offering his very own life — an offer which must be accepted or rejected freely. Thus, the human person is an immense longing quenched only when he or she has surrendered fully to Mystery's all-embracing Spirit of Love.

Moreover, Rahner maintains that our deepest, primordial experience — what haunts the center of our hearts — is of a God who remains Mystery, the Word that illuminates our spirits, and the Love that embraces us. This is not a particular, or "categorical," experience to which we can point. As the "horizon" in which all our experiences take place, it is beyond all particular experiences. One should not even call it *an* experience because it is "transcendental" experience, the ground of all experiences. It is the atmosphere in which we live, our basal spiritual metabolism, "more intimate to us than we are to ourselves," as the mystics were fond of saying. Just as we take for granted our breathing, our beating hearts, or our own self-awareness, so too might the ever-present experience of God remain overlooked, repressed, or even denied. In our daily lives we often overlook or take for granted the divine life we in fact live and experience.

In God's self-communication, we actually experience God-above-us (Mystery), God-with-us (enfleshed Word), and God-in-us (Holy Spirit). The call of Mystery explains why our questions never cease, why we eventually must ask ultimate questions, and why we are never satisfied totally with any-thing in this life. Because we are *historical* persons, we search incessantly for that one person or thing that will fulfill us perfectly — whom Rahner names the "absolute savior." The attraction of the Holy Spirit explains why our immense long-ing often draws us into the deepest levels of our being. Thus, we are essentially *ec*-static beings drawn to God's mystery, worldly and historical beings attracted to an absolute savior, and *en*-static beings drawn to our deepest interior by the fontal fullness of the Spirit of Love.

Because Rahner accentuates the Trinity as Christianity's es-sential mystery, he chides Christians for their often implicit Unitarianism. "One might," he complains, "almost dare to af-firm that if the doctrine of the Trinity were to be erased as false, most religious literature could be preserved almost unchanged throughout the process."[31] To Rahner, however, "no Christian can seriously deny that there is an understanding of the doc-trine of the Trinity in terms of the economy of salvation, that there is an experience of the history of salvation and revela-tion of a threefold kind. The history of revelation and salvation brings us up against the ineffable mystery of the incomprehen-sible, unoriginated God who is called Father, who does not live and remain in metaphysical remoteness, but who seeks in all his incomprehensibility and sovereignty and freedom to im-part himself to the creature as its eternal life in truth and love. This one and incomprehensible God is unsurpassably close to human beings historically in Jesus Christ, who is not simply one prophet in a still continuing series of prophets but the final and unsurpassable self-promise of this one God in history. And this one and the same God imparts himself to us in the inner-most center of human existence as Holy Spirit for salvation and for the consummation which is God himself."[32]

In short, the mystery of God has come to us in Jesus Christ and poured his Spirit of love into our hearts. Thereby we are freed from sin and death and will share God's life for eternity. This the Church explicitly lives and celebrates. Thus, Rahner emphasizes that our Christian lives, prayers, and devotions should be explicitly centered on the Father *as Father*, the Son *as Son*, and the Holy Spirit *as Holy Spirit*.

The Ignatian Exercises focus on giving those making them a deep interior tasting and savoring of the Christian mysteries. In a way these Exercises function "mystagogically," that is, they initiate people into their foundational experience of the triune God. Rahner's theology — with its often mystagogical, theopoetical language — attempts to evoke, to awaken, to deepen, and to strengthen the basic experience of the triune God that haunts every person's core. Redolent with Ignatius's experience of the triune God, Rahner's theology often begins and ends on a mystagogical note: the *experience* of one's lived, root unity of self-possessing knowledge and love penetrated by God's self-communication as mystery, revelation, and love. Ignatius's influence clarifies why most of Rahner's theology evokes the experience of God's self-communication through Christ in the Spirit.[33]

Seeking and Finding God's Will

St. Ignatius writes that "by the term Spiritual Exercises we mean every method of examination of conscience, meditation, contemplation, vocal or mental prayer, and other spiritual activities.... For, just as taking a walk, traveling on foot, and running are physical exercises, so is the name of spiritual exercises given to any means of preparing and disposing our soul to rid itself of all its disordered affections, of seeking and finding God's will in the ordering of our life for the salvation of our soul" (*Exercises*, no. 1).

"During these Spiritual Exercises," Ignatius daringly says, "when a person is seeking God's will, it is more appropriate and far better that the Creator and Lord himself should communicate himself to the devout soul, embracing it in love and praise, and disposing it for the way which will enable the soul to serve him better in the future" (*Exercises*, no. 15). Thus, the Ignatian Exercises focus on the exercitant's experience of God insofar as this enables the person to seek and to find God's specific will for him. They make the astonishing claim that God wills something specific for the individual, and that this will should be sought and can be found in and through the Exercises.

In line with mainstream commentators on the Ignatian Exercises, Rahner describes them as a time of *solitude* and *prayer* to foster *decision* and *choice*. Because the human person is never a mere function of a community, not even of the Church, the Exercises require a person to accept himself or herself in one's ultimate, permanent solitude before God. They expose flight into the masses — even ecclesial ones — and discourage it. Thus, as Rahner says, "the Exercises are *essentially* exercises for *individuals*."[34]

He also adds that "the Exercises are exercises in choice and decision *before God, to God,* and *in Christ,* otherwise they are not exercises."[35] Thus, the exercitant must ask of the triune God in Christ what decision she should make concerning a choice of a way of life or particular changes in her present life. Rahner takes Ignatius's own example quite seriously, for this was a saint who prized deep religious experience not for its own sake but for its ability to reveal God's will to him, a saint who was convinced that his Exercises would allow others to find God's specific will for them. "The Exercises," Rahner says, "presuppose that there is an existential decision through an individual call of God to the actual person."[36]

The Exercises do not indoctrinate. They do not import something from the outside of which the person has no experience; rather, they evoke and intensify the primordial experience of God living in everyone's heart. As Rahner says, "they therefore presuppose and existentially *put into practice* the fundamental substance of Christianity: that the living, incomprehensible God exists, that we have a personal relationship with him in freedom and by grace, a relationship which despite all mediation (through and in Christ, and from Christ through the whole width of earthly existence) is immediate (*on both sides*), that this relationship to God in prayer and decision can and must become thematic and is not just the unthematic, hidden ground of a relationship to the world."[37]

In other words, the initiation of a person through the Exercises into a personally accepted Christianity in faith, hope, and love must also illuminate his or her concrete situation in the world as one of decision. The Exercises awaken both Christianity as a whole *and* a personal decision grounded in it. "The Exercises are and remain choice and decision in a concrete life situation" to Rahner, "because the basic, total *metanoia* . . . is possible only in the concrete life situation and that situation's origin in decision."[38] True Christians must decide — and this on the basis of the Christianity they live.

Rahner views the human person as spirit-in-world, that is, as a worldly being open in knowledge and love to God's mystery. Thus, if the Exercises truly awaken a person to his or her primordial experience of God, they must also awaken the person to the real concrete questions of his or her life. The person "will [then] come to know what is really meant by God, sin, grace, forgiveness, Christ, discipleship of Christ, and the cross only in a question of actual existence posed concretely, faced squarely and not brushed aside, and accepted in free responsibility."[39]

"The Spiritual Exercises are not," to Rahner, "a theological system. From a theological point of view, the Spiritual Exercises are nothing but an election or choice: the choice of the means and the concrete way in which Christianity can become a living reality in us. St. Ignatius is interested only in this: that a man place himself before the Lord of the 'Kingdom of Christ' and the 'Two Standards' and ask: *What should I do?* What do You want from me according to the sovereignty of Your divine will?"[40]

Ignatius assumes that those earnestly seeking God's will make themselves "indifferent to all created things, in regard to everything which is left to our free will and is not forbidden" (*Exercises*, no. 23). By meditating upon and contemplating the life, death, and resurrection of Jesus Christ, the exercitant should so fall in love with the triune Christ that all created things are seen only in the light of this love. Rahner views Ignatian *indiferençia* as the "calm readiness for every command of God, the equanimity which, out of the realization that God is always greater than anything we can experience of him or wherein we can find him, continually detaches itself from every determinate thing which man is tempted to regard as *the* point in which alone God meets him. Hence the characteristic of Ignatian piety... is an ultimate reserve and coolness towards all particular ways because all possession of God must leave God as greater beyond all possession of him. Out of such an attitude of *indiferençia* there springs of itself the perpetual readiness to hear a new call from God to tasks other than those previously engaged in, continually to decamp from those fields where one wanted to find God and to serve him there...[and the] courage to regard no way to him as being *the* way, but rather to seek him in all ways....In brief: such *indiferença* becomes a seeking of God in *all* things. Because God is greater than everything, he can be found if one flees from the world, but he can come to meet one on the streets in the midst of the world. For this reason Ignatius acknowledges only one law in his restless search for God: to seek him in all things,...to seek him in that spot where at any particular time he wants to be found,...to seek him in the world if he wants to show himself in it." Both to Ignatius and to Rahner only someone wholly open to God and free from self-love can seek and find God's will. This is *indiferença* and "the basic structure of the spiritual life."[41]

Ignatius describes briefly three "times" that are suitable for the "election," or the decision regarding God's will. "*The First Time* is an occasion when God our Lord moves and attracts the will in such a way that a devout person, without doubting or being able to doubt, carries out what was proposed. This is what St. Paul and St. Matthew did when they followed Christ our Lord. *The Second Time* is present when sufficient clarity and knowledge are received from the experience of consolations and desolations, and from experience in the discernment of various spirits. *The Third Time* is one of tranquillity...when the soul is not being moved one way and the other by various spirits and uses its natural faculties in freedom and peace" (nos. 175–77). Rahner contends that Ignatius "regards the second time for Election as the usual one...that Ignatius not only had an unmistakable preference for the second mode of Election in his own life, but also recommended its use to others."[42]

Rahner presupposes that a person during the Exercises will experience in differing intensities a wide variety of disturbing and consoling thoughts, desires, emotions, and moods. How can the exercitant discern which of these truly come from God and thus should be followed? Which come from "the enemy of our human nature" and thus should be rejected? It is especially during the second time of election that one must indeed discern the various spirits.

The key to the discernment of spirits, to Rahner, is what Ignatius calls "consolation without previous cause." Ignatius says that "only God our Lord can give the soul consolation without a preceding cause. For it is the prerogative of the Creator alone to enter the soul, depart from it, and cause a motion in it which draws the whole person into the love of His Divine Majesty.... When the consolation is without preceding cause there is no deception in it, since it is coming only from God our Lord" (nos. 330 and 336). When God *alone* consoles, he moves the soul in precisely *this* way. This God-given movement, for Rahner, is the "first principle" of Ignatius's "supernatural logic."[43] God lays hold of the soul completely, opens it in a way in which it is not generally open, and bestows upon the person a supreme and irresistible certitude. This God-given consolation cannot deceive because God effects a pure openness to him, an *indiferençia* of the highest quality, which draws the person *wholly* into God's love.

To Rahner, the person who receives this unique consolation from God during the Exercises has the criterion for judging all other motions in the soul. Those motions that enhance or are congruent with it are indications of God's will; those that disturb this attunement to God are counter-indicative.

For example, presuppose that a person during the Exercises wishes to discover God's will concerning his somewhat weak attraction to the priesthood. The person prays the Exercises and experiences not only conflicting thoughts, desires, emotions, and moods but also consolation without previous cause. Let us further assume that whenever the person presents his desire to become a priest before the Lord, he experiences a profound joy and peace, that is, a harmony between his *fundamental* religious attitude — openness to God — and the object of choice, the priesthood.

For Ignatius and Rahner, this is a sign that God wants the person to become a priest. As Rahner says, "the real signs of the congruence and coherence of the two factors which are confronted with one another in the Second Mode of Election are... peace, joy, tranquillity, quiet, gladness, interior joy, warmth and fervor. It is precisely from them that it is to be recognized whether the object in question in the Election is good or bad. But all these signs are only aspects of what we have called congruence between the divine consolation and the prospective putting of oneself in the situation of having chosen a certain object [the priesthood], or between the fundamental religious attitude and the particular decision. And this congruence is to be understood as experienced by the exercitant."[44] In our case, the object of choice, the at first vague desire for the priesthood, enhances the person's innermost openness to God. It is in harmony with it and brings the person an increase of joy, love, and peace. The person experiences more deeply his love for God in the context of deciding about the priesthood. To decide to become a priest is then the practical means of expressing his love for God. It is congruent with this love and will bring him joy and peace. In short, his decision "feels" at one with his love for God; it feels right.

The experience of consolation without previous cause, to Rahner, can occur on very different levels and with differing degrees of intensity. The lowest stage occurs when we experience ourselves as a self-transcending insatiable hunger dissatisfied with all created things. This immense yearning is a fundamental, global awareness of self and contains an awareness of God. We often makes decisions on the basis of this *deepest* hunger because it "feels" right deep down. To be sure, we often decide in the light of our superficial and disordered hungers. Even then, however, deep within our being it still doesn't "feel" right. Ignatius's logic of existential decision, therefore, should concern nearly everyone.

Rahner states boldly: "It may be said too that *nearly everyone* in grave decisions makes a choice more or less exactly in the way Ignatius conceives it, just as the man in the street uses logic without ever having studied it, and yet it remains useful to draw inferences by means of logic that one has studied. In such decisions a man thinks things over for a long time. Consequently in every case he will probably make his decisions through a fundamental global awareness of himself actually present and making itself felt in him during this space of time, and through a feeling of the harmony or disharmony of the object of choice with this fundamental feeling he has about himself. He will not only nor ultimately make his decision by a rational analysis but by whether he feels that something 'suits him' or not. And this feeling will be judged by whether the matter pleases, delights, brings peace and satisfaction.... Is his [Ignatius's] teaching not the elaborated technique, worked out into its essentials, of what the faithful do by and large every day but with a greater risk of gross failures?"[45]

For this reason Rahner considers Ignatius to be as important for the Church as Aristotle is for the field of philosophy. Through Aristotle logic became the first science of philosophy; through Ignatius, the logic of existential decision became the science of the saints concerning Christian existence.

A Communal Logic of Existential Decision

In the light of contemporary studies on the founding of the Society of Jesus, Rahner notes that Ignatius did not regard himself as the sole founder of his Order.[46] United as a community by the spirit of the Exercises, he and his first companions founded the Order through a deliberation that occurred not only in the group but *of* the group. Through a dialectical process of shared testing and decision making, Ignatius's Exercises took place dynamically in and for a community.

One might argue that the first "conciliar" decision of the primitive Church concerning the observance of the Mosaic law by pagan converts was reached through this communal discernment of spirits, a decision which "seemed good to the apostles and the elders, with the whole church" (Acts 15:22). One might further argue that the great councils of the Christian Church ultimately reached their decisions through a deliberation *of* the community as a self-expression of a community in the discernment of spirits and the act of choice.

Rahner notes that in our age the Church should look to higher forms of socialization. He argues that communal acts of decision which occur in the religious context of the discernment of spirits and involve the Ignatian rules of choice can be done by "basic communities," religious Orders, secular institutes, parish councils, the college of bishops, and the like. In short, Rahner believes that a genuinely collective discernment of spirits is possible and necessary for the contemporary Church at all levels.

Although Rahner states that the "special quality of the Ignatian Exercises can be expressed in the new form of a collective retreat as the self-expression of the Church," he does not see the traditional solitary retreat "losing its worth."[47] Why? Because the human person, to Rahner, is always a unique individual and a social being. Hence, "the acceptance and the existential and religious interpretation of loneliness in the face of the mystery we call God, whose very silence is a mode of speech, form an essential part of individual retreats and can only be properly dealt with in this context and not in group retreats.... Men without the courage to pray privately could scarcely be members and representatives of a society containing higher forms of socialization as these are being sought today."[48]

Existential Ethics

The Church's essentialist ethics concerns itself with universal moral principles, everywhere and always valid. This ethics therefore explicates the laws written into universal human nature and emphasizes that certain actions are intrinsically good or evil for all persons.

Rahner understands the human person to be more than a particular instance of a universal human nature. He sees each person as more than *a* man or *a* woman, but instead in some respect as an utterly and absolutely unique individual. To Rahner, human beings differ from each other not only by material delimitation (as in the way no two snowflakes are alike) but because each is uniquely spirit, an ineffable individual.

Some decisions, therefore, are good or evil depending upon the unique person because of God's unique will for that individual. Rahner's reflection on Ignatius's supernatural logic of decision becomes explicit in his work on existential ethics, which contends that human decisions must sometimes be made in a way that transcends (but does not contradict) the application of general and universal principles.[49] An existential ethics — the way of finding the existential ethical imperative "you must do this" — is at the heart of Ignatius's Exercises.

In line with this, Rahner also makes an important distinction between principles which express a universal essence and prescriptions which are directed to the concrete particular.[50] He chides the official Church and some Christians for talking too much about abstract unchanging principles and not enough about prescriptions. Unlike Ignatius, they choose an abstract end and neglect decisions concerning the concrete means to attaining a provisional but quite definite goal. Unlike principles, prescriptions are neither always and absolutely true nor always and absolutely false. Ignatius did not hesitate to make provisional decisions, to decide in the light of his experience of God that he must do this or that, at least in the short run. Why doesn't the Church have a "game plan" for the next fifty years? The official Church, Christian groups, and individual Christians should have a concrete program of Christian action. Given the current situation in the world, in Germany, and in the individual Christian's life, Rahner asks: what should Christians at various levels *do?*

The Christological Basis of Ignatian Logic

Rahner was once criticized for neglecting the Christological dimension of the Ignatian logic of existential decision. His reply underscores that the Ignatian Exercises place the decision in the context of meditations and contemplations on Christ's life, death, or resurrection.[51] To Rahner, all grace is the grace of Jesus Christ. Thus, the conditions requisite for such a decision bear the stamp of Christ's grace. Most importantly, the *indiferençia* requisite for this decision is a real participation in Christ's death. As Rahner says, "A person can choose or reject a particular object only if he has, by the grace of God, freed himself from an immediate attachment to this object and has thus achieved openness to immediacy to God as the sole focus of his existence. This detachment, not merely theoretical but existential, from a particular finite value, is in all truth...a participation in Christ's death. Only Christ, crucified and risen, guarantees that such a dying is possible and that it is not after all merely the descent into the void of absurdity.... This 'dying,' which is a basic element in every Christian choice, takes place in the grace of Christ together with Christ, whether we explicitly know it or not. It reaches its climax and perfect victory in real death, if one dies 'in the Lord,' just as it got its start in one's being baptized 'into the death of Christ.' "[52]

An Architectonic Theology

Ignatius's mystical transformation on the banks of the river Cardoner bestowed upon him an "architectonic," or holistic, comprehension of the unity-in-diversity of the Christian faith. In becoming a new man with a new mind, he grasped the fundamental oneness of the Christian faith, the essential cohesion and coherence of the individual mysteries of faith. Through his spirituality, Rahner experienced this oneness and inner cohesion of the Christian faith. To him, "there is an *experience* of grace, and this is the real, fundamental reality of Christianity itself."[53] Rahner experienced in prayer that Christianity is something total and single that can be accepted or denied only in its totality.

About Thomas Aquinas, Rahner wrote that the saint "always thinks on the basis of the whole and in relation to the whole."[54] Thus Rahner's architectonic grasp of Christianity — inspired in part by Ignatius's Cardoner experience — led him to theologize from Christianity's core. His theology attempts to explicate Christianity as the "*one single* aperture which leads out of all the individual truths (and even errors) into *the* truth which is the unique incomprehensibility of God."[55] Simply stated, Christianity to Rahner is nothing more than the "awakening and interpretation of the most interior aspect in the human person, of the ultimate depth of his existence."[56] On the basis of the long history of salvation which reached its high point in Jesus Christ, Christianity in essence is the best interpretation of what we are in essence: forgiven and loved by God and called to love each other.

The holistic view of the faith Rahner assimilated from Ignatius may also explain his concern for "short formulas of the faith."[57] In only a few sentences these brief creedal statements attempt to explain Christianity's essence to a contemporary person. What is perhaps his most important short formula elucidates the intimate link — even unity — between love of God, of neighbor, and of self.[58] To Rahner, the more deeply we experience God, the more deeply we experience our own identity. He writes: "The history of the experience of self, i.e., of man's interpretation of himself as achieved in freedom, is *eo ipso* the experience of the history of God as well, and *vice versa.*"[59]

Genuine love of neighbor, to Rahner, *is* love of God. "We must acknowledge," he writes, "that the act of loving God is closely related to the act of loving our neighbor, that *these acts are mutually coexistent.* We should always bear in mind that the God in all his reality to whom we reach out through freely given acts of love is a God of love, of supremely free love. Hence we cannot accept and affirm him simply by loving him; we must also freely love and accept all other spiritual beings to whom he lovingly reveals himself.... In other words, the persons we love form a direct line of communication to God. The world is always the starting point for our relationship to God because we can only build up this relationship freely and consciously out of our own finite existence.... If we take 'human being' instead of 'world' as our starting point, bearing in mind that one can only realize one's true being, freely responsible to God, with the help of one's fellow men, we can say that the person who is the object of our love is the real mediator in our relationship to God, that through him or her we achieve direct contact with God."[60]

One can love God whom one does not see only by loving one's visible neighbor. In Ignatian terms radical love of neighbor demands the self-forgetting requisite for *indiferença,* radical openness to God. In a powerful meditation written for the feast of St. Ignatius, Rahner writes that the person of genuine *indiferença* becomes homeless in the true sense.[61] Homeless in God's incomprehensibility, the person of *indiferença* identifies more easily with society's marginal people.

However, Rahner also reverses the emphases because God "is what is most intimate, the essential kernel of the beloved being, he is within even the inmost, the least relative, the ultimate enclosure of man himself.... Whoever loves such a God, whoever casts his whole being into God, in love and adoration and submission... is by that fact in the innermost kernel of the loved man. He has penetrated behind the ultimate mystery of that man, because he has reached where God is.... Now we can understand why only he who loves God can love his brother... because a direct love for a man cannot penetrate efficaciously and creatively to that point where the man is in reality and properly 'himself.' "[62]

The person who tries to love another human being will

soon discover human sinfulness, which is unlovable. But any-one, whether believer or unbeliever, who genuinely loves the other, gets beyond his own sinfulness and that of the other, and reaches the other's genuine identity, which is ultimately mys-tery, inextricably linked to God's mystery. This loving can be accomplished only by way of a self-surrender which is in fact (if not in name) genuine worship of God. Similarly, only some-one who loves God radically, even if only implicitly, can truly love another human being. More about this important topic will be said later on in different contexts.

The Priesthood

In a profound article on the spirituality and essence of priest-hood, Rahner says that St. Ignatius of Loyola wanted both to be ordained a priest and to found an Order of priests. "How-ever," he writes, "... this was simply because, for him, it was concretely the most practical way and the condition of the pos-sibility of getting on with what he really wanted to do. In his own spirituality he was not at all terribly insistent about saying Mass; if I remember rightly, he waited a whole year after his ordination before he got as far as that, but then he said Mass very gladly and with immense devotion. But with his first com-panions he went into prisons and ministered to the sick. For him it was enormously important to be in the closest possible contact with the poor and the socially underprivileged of his time in the prisons and to go into the hideous hospitals of that period, to convert prostitutes in Rome, perhaps also to run a school to inspire pious princesses, etc. In a word, what he in fact did seems open to the inane verdict or objection that it could all have been achieved by people who were not priests. Against this, it must be pointed out that precisely in view of historical variability and of theology it is impossible to describe anything as properly and solely priestly, as what *only* the priest can do. That is to say: preaching the Gospel, ministering to the poor, defending the underprivileged, following Jesus in this sense, prayer, a mystical sphere of one's own existence, are just as much part of the priestly office as — and I do not mean it in a pejorative sense — 'being able to say Mass.' "[63]

St. Ignatius's influence may also account for Rahner's emphasis not only on what the priest does but also on what the priest *is* — that is, his stress not only on priestly function but also on priestly *existence*.

However, Rahner does not seem to comprehend that Ignatius postponed his First Mass for a year to prepare himself better to say it and with the hope of celebrating it in the Holy Land. Ignatius also used this period to beg the Eternal Father "to place him with his Son." Ignatius contended that one must live or be like an angel to be even somewhat worthy to say Mass. Not only did Ignatius say Mass "gladly and with immense devotion," but the Mass also became the central place for his extraordinary mystical life.

Concluding Summary

The phrase, "to be with Christ to serve," may summarize Ignatian spirituality. Rahner took seriously the solitary side of Ignatius's mysticism which took place in self-emptying, silence, and contemplation.[64] However, Ignatius's intimacy with the triune Christ expressed itself in apostolic service. As Rahner underscores, "in earthly man this emptying of self will not be accomplished by practicing pure inwardness, but by real activity which is called humility, service, love of neighbor, the cross and death. One must descend into hell together with Christ and lose one's soul, not directly to the God who is above all names, but in the service of one's brethren."[65] Thus, Rahner distrusted any spirituality which renounced the world too quickly or ended up in an impersonal Absolute.

Rahner claims that the Ignatian formula "finding God in all things" is "the attempt of the mystic to translate his experience for others and make them share in his grace."[66] This can likewise be said of almost all Rahner's theology. Some commentators contend that Rahner's pious and spiritual writings are the overflow or the application of his speculative theology. However, to the extent that this is true, it can be argued that his philosophical and theological writings were decisively influenced by his own Ignatian religious experiences and that of St. Ignatius. That his philosophy and theology, for the most part, attempt to explicate what is intrinsic to these experiences explains the Ignatian flavor redolent throughout Rahner's writings.

For Rahner, philosophy "is properly speaking a theology that has not yet arrived at the fullness of its own nature."[67] "The depths of the human abyss," he writes, "in a thousand ways is *the* theme of philosophy, is already the abyss which has been opened by God's grace and which stretches into the depths of God himself."[68]

Thus an Ignatian mystical eros permeates the roots of Rahner's philosophical and theological enterprise. What Rahner says about Thomas Aquinas can also be said of his own theology: "Thomas' theology is his spiritual life and his spiritual life is his theology."[69] The power, authenticity, and attractiveness of Rahner's theology issues from the philosophical and theological reflection upon his own Ignatian spirituality. With Johann B. Metz we can say that Rahner's theology is a "type of existential biography, . . . a mystical biography of religious experience, of the history of a life before the veiled face of God, in the doxology of faith."[70]

Notes

1. See *The Spiritual Exercises of Saint Ignatius of Loyola,* trans. and commentary George E. Ganss, S.J. (St. Louis: Institute of Jesuit Sources, 1992).

2. *Karl Rahner in Dialogue,* 191.

3. *Faith in a Wintry Season,* 96.

4. Trans. Kenneth Baker, S.J. (New York: Herder and Herder, 1965).

5. Trans. Edward Quinn (New York: Seabury Press, 1973).

6. "Ignatius of Loyola Speaks to a Modern Jesuit," *Ignatius of Loyola,* historical introduction by Paul Imhof, S.J., trans. Rosaleen Ockenden (Cleveland: Collins, 1978), 11–38.

7. *Faith in a Wintry Season,* 104.

8. Ibid., 40.

9. *The Priesthood,* 281.

10. "Erfahrungen eines katholischen Theologen," *Vor dem Geheimnis Gottes den Menschen Verstehen,* ed. Karl Lehmann (Munich: Verlag Schnell & Steiner, 1984), 114. My emphasis.

11. "The Logic of Concrete Individual Knowledge in Ignatius Loyola," in *The Dynamic Element in the Church,* trans. W. J. O'Hara (New York: Herder and Herder, 1964), 86–87, n. 1.

12. "Reflections on a New Task for Fundamental Theology," *Theological Investigations XVI*, trans. David Morland, O.S.B. (New York: Crossroad Publishing Co., 1979), 166. Henceforth references to the *Theological Investigations* will be abbreviated as *TI*, followed by the volume number.

13. "Being Open to God as Ever Greater," *TI VII*, trans. David Bourke (New York: Herder and Herder, 1971), 25–46.

14. "Modern Piety and the Experience of Retreats," *TI XVI*, 138.

15. "The Ignatian Process for Discovering the Will of God in an Existential Situation: Some Theological Problems in the Rules for Election and Discernment of Spirits in St. Ignatius's *Spiritual Exercises*," *Ignatius of Loyola: His Personality and Spiritual Heritage, 1556–1956*, ed. Friedrich Wulf, S.J. (St. Louis: Institute of Jesuit Sources, 1977), 280–89.

16. "The Logic of Concrete Individual Knowledge in Ignatius Loyola," *The Dynamic Element in the Church*, 85–87.

17. *Karl Rahner in Dialogue*, 292; "Reflections on a New Task for Fundamental Theology," *TI XVI*, 165–66; "On the Question of a Formal Existential Ethics," *TI II*, trans. Karl-H. Kruger (Baltimore: Helicon Press, 1964), 231–32.

18. "Reflections on a New Task for Fundamental Theology," *TI XVI*, 165–66.

19. *Karl Rahner in Dialogue*, 196.

20. *TI XVI*, x.

21. "Erfahrungen eines katholischen Theologen," *Vor dem Geheimnis Gottes den Menschen Verstehen*, 114.

22. *TI XVI*, viii.

23. *Faith in a Wintry Season*, 161.

24. "Rede des Ignatius von Loyola an einen Jesuiten von Heute," *Schriften zur Theologie XV* (Zürich: Benziger Verlag, 1983), 373–77. For an alternate English translation, see "Ignatius of Loyola Speaks to a Modern Jesuit," *Ignatius of Loyola*, 11–15.

25. "Mystical Experience and Mystical Theology," *TI XVII*, trans. Margaret Kohl (New York: Crossroad Publishing Co., 1981), 97, n. 8.

26. *Karl Rahner in Dialogue*, 211.

27. "The Experience of God Today," *TI XI*, trans. David Bourke (New York: Seabury Press, 1974), 159–60.

28. *The Trinity*, trans. Joseph Donceel (New York: Herder and Herder, 1970).

29. "The Hiddenness of God," *TI XVI*, 240.

30. This states less technically Rahner's theory of the "supernatural existential." See Karl Rahner and Herbert Vorgrimler, *Dictionary of*

Theology, new revised edition (New York: Crossroad Publishing Co., 1981), 163–64.

31. "Remarks on the Dogmatic Treatise 'De Trinitate,'" *TI IV*, trans. Kevin Smyth (Baltimore: Helicon Press, 1966), 79.

32. "Oneness and Threefoldness of God in Discussion with Islam," *TI XVIII*, trans. Edward Quinn (New York: Crossroad Publishing Co., 1983), 114.

33. See "The Concept of Mystery in Catholic Theology," *TI IV*, esp. 60–73.

34. "The *Exercises* Today," *Christian at the Crossroads,* trans. V. Green (New York: Seabury, 1975), 71.

35. Ibid., 70.

36. Ibid.

37. Ibid.

38. Ibid., 72–73.

39. Ibid., 73.

40. *Spiritual Exercises,* 11–12. My emphases.

41. *The Priesthood,* 30. Also see 30–38.

42. "The Logic of Concrete Individual Knowledge in Ignatius Loyola," *The Dynamic Element in the Church,* 96–97, n. 11.

43. Ibid., 130.

44. Ibid., 162–63.

45. Ibid., 166–67.

46. "Modern Piety and the Experience of Retreats," *TI XVI*, 135–55. For the source of the remarks that follow, see esp. 145–55.

47. Ibid., 154.

48. Ibid., 155.

49. "On the Question of a Formal Existential Ethics," *TI II*, 217–34.

50. For the sources of the remarks which follow, see "Principles and Prescriptions," *The Dynamic Element in the Church,* 13–41; "Do Not Evade Decisions!" *Everyday Faith,* trans. W. J. O'Hara (New York: Herder and Herder, 1968), 135–41.

51. See "Comments by Karl Rahner on Questions Raised by Avery Dulles," trans. James M. Quigley, S.J., *Ignatius of Loyola: His Personality and Spiritual Heritage, 1556–1956,* 290–93.

52. Ibid., 292.

53. "Theology and Anthropology," *TI IX*, trans. Graham Harrison (New York: Seabury Press, 1972), 41.

54. "Thomas Aquinas: Patron of Theological Studies," *The Great Church Year,* 316.

55. "Intellectual Honesty and Christian Faith," *TI VII*, 61.

56. "The Theological Dimension of the Question about Man," *TI XVII*, 67.

57. One finds in Rahner's *Foundations of Christian Faith* (trans. William V. Dych, S.J. [New York: Seabury Press, 1978]), 448–59, three such formulas. One brief creedal statement states: "A person really discovers his true self in a genuine act of self-realization only if he risks himself radically for another. If he does this, he grasps unthematically or explicitly what we mean by God as the horizon, the guarantor and the radical depths of his love, the God who in his personal and historical self-communication made himself the realm in which such love is possible. This love is meant in both an interpersonal and a social sense, and in the radical unity of both these elements it is the ground and essence of the church" (456). Also see "The Need for a 'Short Formula' of the Christian Faith," *TI IX*, 117–26; "Reflections on the Problems Involved in Devising a Short Formula of the Faith," *TI XI*, 230–44.

58. See "The Experience of Self and Experience of God," *TI XIII*, trans. David Bourke (New York: Seabury Press, 1975), 122–32; "The 'Commandment' of Love in Relation to the Other Commandments," *TI V*, trans. Karl-H. Kruger (Baltimore: Helicon Press, 1966), 439–59; "Reflections of the Unity of the Love of Neighbor and the Love of God," *TI VI*, trans. Karl-H. and Boniface Kruger (Baltimore: Helicon Press, 1969), 231–49.

59. "The Experience of Self and Experience of God," *TI XIII*, 131.

60. Karl Rahner and Johann B. Metz, *The Courage to Pray*, trans. Sarah O'Brien Twohig (New York: Crossroad Publishing Co., 1981), 55–56.

61. See "Ignatius of Loyola," *The Great Church Year*, 329–40.

62. "The Consecration of the Layman to the Care of Souls," *TI III*, trans. Karl-H. and Boniface Kruger (Baltimore: Helicon, 1967), 271.

63. "Spirituality of the Priest in the Light of his Office," *TI XIX*, trans. Edward Quinn (New York: Crossroad Publishing Co., 1983), 124.

64. *Karl Rahner in Dialogue*, 142 and 183.

65. *Visions and Prophecies*, trans. Charles Henkey and Richard Strachan (New York: Herder and Herder, 1963), 14, n. 12.

66. "The Logic of Concrete Individual Knowledge in Ignatius Loyola," *The Dynamic Element in the Church*, 155.

67. "On the Current Relationship between Philosophy and Theology," *TI XIII*, 65.

68. "Philosophy and Theology," *TI VI*, 78.

69. "Thomas Aquinas: Patron of Theological Studies," *The Great Church Year*, 316.

70. Johann B. Metz, "Karl Rahner — ein theologisches Leben," *Stimmen der Zeit* (May 1974): 308.

Chapter 3

Karl Rahner — Mystical Theologian

In the previous chapter we saw that Rahner's theological point of departure is God's *self*-communication to the human person whose deepest meaning is to be the addressee of this self-communication. Because of this irrevocable relationship between God and the human person, Rahner contends that theology is anthropology, and vice versa. Thus, to say something about God is to say something about the human being; to say something about the human being is to say something about God.

We also saw that God's self-communication to *all* persons is experiential. Despite the complete gratuity of God's self-communication, Rahner considers the experience of God to be a human "existential," that is, an aspect of the human being precisely as human. Thus, all persons experience God, though often only in a hidden way. Moreover, the free, conscious, and self-conscious person does not experience God sporadically but constantly. I would argue that the experience of grace — that is, God's self-communication at the heart of human existence — summarizes Rahner's entire theological enterprise. He is the preeminent theologian of experienced grace.

Rahner underscores that we live in a seemingly atheistic age, an age of the death of God. Contemporary science and technology have given men and women the ability to control and change not only the world, but even themselves. Even one's interior life is subject to scientific exploration. The theoretical and practical atheism of our age, however, has also contributed to the destruction of false images of God. To Rahner, God is first and foremost not *a* being, but the incomprehensible ground of being. Moreover, God is the personal, holy, and loving Mystery whom one must address as "Thou."

Personal Relationship to God

To Rahner, the primary and essential factor in contemporary Christian life is one's direct personal relationship with God. Thus, anyone who opens the depths of his or her being to God's incomprehensibility despite public opinion and customs, "anyone who manages to live with this incomprehensible and silent God is already practicing devout Christian living."[1]

If we are to have the courage to enter into a direct relationship with the ineffable, incomprehensible God, then "we do need to work out a certain theology of mysticism, a mysticism that leads to a religious experience which indeed many suppose that they could never discover in themselves, a theology of mysticism which can be imparted in such a way that each one can become his own teacher of mysticism."[2] The mystical approach of which Rahner speaks should evoke a person's primordial experience of God. From there one can form a correct image of God as the incomprehensible, yet loving and personal, One to whom one can say "Thou." "The mystical approach of which we have been speaking must teach us in the concrete to maintain a constant closeness to *this* God; to say 'thou' to him, to commit ourselves to his silence and darkness."[3] "It must be made intelligible to people," Rahner says, "that they have an implicit but true knowledge of God — perhaps not reflected upon and not verbalized; or better expressed, they have a genuine experience of God ultimately rooted in their spiritual existence, in their transcendentality, in their personality, or whatever you want to call it."[4] This provides the context for understanding what Rahner said on numerous occasions, namely, that "the devout Christian of the future will either be a 'mystic,' one who has experienced 'something,' or he will cease to be anything at all."[5]

One can and perhaps should avoid the term "mysticism," however, because of its almost unavoidable association with strange, singular, psychic phenomena which have nothing to do with "normal" Christian life.[6] The reality of the experience of God in daily life — not the term used for it — matters to Rahner. "In the final analysis," he says, "it is unimportant whether you call such a personal, genuine experience of God, which occurs in the deepest core of a person, 'mystical.'"[7] However, Rahner does often speak of the "mystical" dimension of Christianity and of the mystical depths of the human being. For example, because "we do have an immediate, preconceptual experience of God through the experience of the limitless breadth of our consciousness," he says, "there is such a thing as a mystical component to Christianity."[8] In fact, "mysticism as the experience of grace,"[9] to him, grounds not only the ordinary Christian's life of faith, hope, and love but also that of anyone living according to his or her conscience.

Thus, Rahner seemingly identifies mysticism as the primordial experience of God in every human life. From a Rahnerian perspective, therefore, the human person is *homo mysticus*, mystical man. Because the person is the addressee of God's self-communication, all personal experiences contain at least an implicit, yet primordial, experience of God. In fact, all human experiences, to Rahner, tend toward "an intensification which is directed towards something which one could in fact call mystical experience."[10] Thus, each and every human being's experience of immense longing for complete happiness contains within itself the seeds of mysticism. Strictly speaking, therefore, everyone is at least a sleeping, distracted, or repressed mystic. To deny this experience with one's entire being — not simply with words — is to deny one's deepest self. It is damnation.

The Mysticism of Everyday Life

Since all genuine faith, hope, and love contain a primordial experience of God, Rahner speaks often of the mysticism of everyday life. Paradoxically, this mysticism normally appears in the grayness and banality of daily life, in contrast to the psychologically dramatic way the mysticism of the great saints is manifested. In fact, we weave the fabric of our eternal lives out of our humdrum days.[11] "If, however, there is such a thing as eternal life at all," Rahner writes, "if it is not merely something different added to our temporal life and likewise stretching out over time, if it is truly the finality of this present life of

freedom which fittingly comes to a final and definitive consummation, only then can we see the unfathomable depths and
richness of our existence, of that existence which often gives the
impression of consisting of nothing but banalities. Where an ultimate responsibility is assumed in obedience to a person's own
conscience, where ultimate selfless love and fidelity are given,
where an ultimate selfless obedience to truth regardless of self
is lived out, and so on, at this point there is really in our life
something that is infinitely precious...that is able to fill out an
eternity."[12]

This mysticism of everyday life encompasses even the most
humble aspects of our daily routine, such as our working,
sleeping, eating, drinking, laughing, seeing, sitting, and getting about. To Rahner, for example, "getting about is one of
the most common everyday activities....We sometimes speak
of a 'walk' or 'way' of life....Christians were at first known
as those 'belonging to the way' (Acts 9:2)....The Bible...tells
us that we must not only live in the Spirit, but 'walk' in the
Spirit....Man's life, too, is often described as a pilgrimage,
and a pilgrimage certainly connotes an uncommon amount
of getting about....This purely physical activity of continually moving from one place to another warns us that we have
here no sure abode....[The Christian] is borne along incessantly by some power conscious of itself and of not having
fulfilled its purpose...ever believing it will find its goal in the
end, because...that goal is God himself towards whose Second Coming, in the person of Christ, our own future moves
inexorably."[13]

Rahner's meditation on eating is also instructive. To him,
"the nutritional process in man transforms food into *human*
stuff, that is, into a being that reflects upon itself, is present to
itself, is master of itself, and in which the world becomes conscious of itself. If, ultimately, the lower can be envisaged only in
terms of the higher,...then we can say that eating is the lowli-
est, although the most noble form of a process (the nutritional
process) whose noblest product is a rational being who gives
himself lovingly and unreservedly to the whole environment
or world which his awareness presents to him....And what
better way is there of symbolizing — or even actually bringing about — a loving, confiding unity among men than eating

together, all sharing in common that bodily nourishment essential to their common existence, and all...opening their hearts to one another? But a meal can stand also as a sign for the final and perfect communion of humanity that will take place at the eternal banquet where the bread that will be eaten and the cup that will be drunk will be the Lord himself. Then indeed will men be truly united to one another and to God."[14]

A genuine Christian who lives the mysticism of daily life possesses the bold, but often hidden, confidence that ordinary daily life is the stuff of authentic life and real Christianity.[15] It is instructive to note how often the words "ordinary," "banal," "humdrum," "routine," and the like show up in Rahner's writings. For him, "grace has its history in man's day-to-day existence with its splendors and failures and is *actually experienced there.*"[16] Rahner urges us to look to our everyday lives to find the presence of God's grace, his loving presence.

For example, Rahner admired St. Ignatius's heroic love of God and his passionate love of Christ's cross and of sharing in the ignominy of Christ's death. The great asceticism of the newly converted Ignatius, his poverty as radical as that of St. Francis, and his extraordinary mystical gifts impressed Rahner. However, because Ignatius had experienced the ever-greater God, he learned to find God in all things. The mature Ignatius directed his attitude of *indiferençia* towards everything, even towards a dramatic carrying of Christ's cross, an attitude that greatly impressed Rahner. The mature Ignatius knew that more often than not God calls us to carry an undramatic cross of Christ. He writes: "The cross, yes, *if* it should please his divine Majesty to call to such a death in life. *Indiferençia* is possible only where the will to a flight from the world is alive, and yet this *indiferençia* in its turn disguises that love for the foolishness of the cross into a daily *moderation* of a *normal style of life* marked by *good sense*. Filled with such *indiferençia*, Ignatius can forgo manifestations of mystical graces — after all God is beyond even the world of experience of the mystic — he can forgo the mystical gift of tears because the physician wanted it — Saint Francis had angrily rejected precisely the same remonstrances of the physician."[17] Thus, because of the way God called Ignatius to serve, the spirituality of the mature Ignatius became less extraordinary, at least in its exterior manifestations.

The Immense Longing

Perhaps the universal experience of the immense longing is the most easily recognized form of the mysticism of everyday life. All persons experience the profound difference between what they want from life and what life actually gives them. Even those who have intelligence, prestige, power, wealth, reputation, health, and a loving family — those who seem to have it all — experience a profound emptiness at times.

The hunger of the heart is revealed in the mistaken belief that the thing or person that will fulfill us totally is just around the corner. We are always on the lookout for the one person or thing we suppose will quench the immense longing that haunts us from the depths of our being. To be human, to Rahner, is to be an immense longing. As a child, we want one toy; as a young person, to belong to the right group, get into the right school, or date the right person; as an adult, to obtain the right position, find the right mate, and the like. Yet when we obtain our heart's alleged desire, we soon discover it is not enough.

The heart is a lonely hunter because it is restless until it rests in God. The immense longing we feel in daily life underscores that nothing finite ultimately satisfies us, that we will settle for nothing less than perfect life and total fulfillment. In fact, the Scriptures tell us that the first temptation was to be like God, indicating that we want it all. The immense longing, for Rahner, points to an either-or situation: either God exists or life is absurd. When asked by an interviewer, "Is there one question that seems to you as a theologian to be perhaps the most important?" Rahner replied: "Yes, there is such a question. It runs like this: Is human existence absurd or does it have an ultimate meaning? If it is absurd, why do human beings have an unquenchable hunger for meaning? Is it not a consequence of God's existence? For if God doesn't exist, then the hunger for meaning is absurd."[18]

Because God has communicated himself to the core of our being, we experience God at least in a silent, hidden, and even repressed way. This ever-present experience of God, the anonymous presence of our heart's desire, is the ambience or horizon against which we experience all else. The God-experience is the cause of our dissatisfaction with life, for nothing measures up

to that which rests at our deepest center. The immense longing speaks to us, even if at times only in a whisper: this or
that finite thing is ultimately not where we have already set our
hearts.

The Mysticism of Joy in the World

The mysticism of everyday life, to Rahner, exists not only as the
immense longing and not only as the undertow, vector, or implicit call to holiness found in every person's deepest interior. It
also becomes more explicit in the many good and lovely experiences that punctuate even the most banal lives. Hence, Rahner
calls attention to joyful experiences, to the good and beautiful
things of life because they "promise and point to eternal light
and everlasting life."[19] Since God can be found in all things,
because God became flesh, there is certainly an Easter faith
that loves the earth, a radical mysticism of joy in the world.[20]
"To such an attitude," Rahner writes, "Ignatian piety and mysticism can lead us. Ignatian affirmation of the world is not a
naive optimism, not an installing of ourselves in the world as
though we had in it the center of our existence. Ignatian joy in
the world springs from the mysticism of conformity with him
whom we have joined in the flight from the world contained in
the foolishness of the cross. But once we have found the God
of the life beyond, then such an attitude will break out of deep
seclusion in God into the world, and work as long as day lasts,
immerse itself in the work of the time in the world and yet
await with deep longing the Coming of the Lord."[21]

In the Gospels, one finds Jesus at wedding feasts, at ban-
quets, changing water into wine, making food available to the
hungry — in short, eating and drinking in a way that shocked
the Pharisees. Jesus marvelled at the birds of the air, the flowers of the field, and rejoiced in the many joys found in ordinary
life. As Rahner says, "The good things in life are not only for
the rascals."[22] To someone for whom the experience of suffering negated God's existence, Rahner countered, "Have you even
once tried to make your experience of happiness, of meaning,
of joy, of shelteredness likewise an argument from which the
presentiment of the eternal God of light and blessedness can
unfold in you?"[23] Yet, Rahner cautions us to distinguish authen-

tic recreation from empty diversion, for only the former signals God's presence in the things of life that renew us spiritually. The good things of life genuinely re-create us, and fill us with joy and peace. They produce the fruits of the Holy Spirit in our lives.

The Mysticism of the Negative Way

Despite Rahner's appreciation of the mysticism of joy in the world, he prefers to "lay special stress on the *via negationis* [negative way]"[24] because here the human spirit experiences its *proper transcendence.*[25] As he says, "the experience of the meaning of innerworldly values, in love, in fidelity, in beauty, in truth, and so on is finite. As such these values are a promise in their positive aspect, while in their finiteness they are an indication that we must always *proceed beyond* these partial experiences, in the hope of this infinite fulfillment."[26]

According to the Fourth Lateran Council, "between the Creator and the creature no similarity can be expressed without including a *greater dissimilarity.*"[27] The "negative way" emphasizes this radical difference between God and creatures. In this view, God is reached best by negation, forgetting, unknowing, in a darkness of spirit supported by nothing of this world.

For Rahner, however, a "burned-out," "tired and disillusioned heart" is not necessarily closer to God than a young and happy one.[28] All too often do both the joys and sorrows of daily life obscure God's presence. Nonetheless, because the human mystery is infinite emptiness and the divine mystery infinite fullness, "wherever space is really left by parting, by death, by renunciation, by apparent emptiness, provided the emptiness that cannot remain such is not filled by the world, or activity, or chatter, or the deadly grief of the world — there God is."[29]

Thus God is experienced most clearly and most intensely in our ordinary and banal everyday existence, "where the graspable contours of our everyday realities break and dissolve."[30] For Rahner, God's presence becomes transparent when the "lights which illuminate the tiny islands of our everyday life go out."[31] The most telling moment, says Rahner, is when everything that props up our life fails. Then we are forced to ask if the inescapable darkness engulfing us is absolute absurdity or a blessed, holy night.

The mysticism of everyday life can be experienced negatively in a variety of ways. The following vintage Rahner quotation illustrates his preference for the negative way in the mysticism of everyday life, or what he sometimes calls the experience of the Spirit: "I can now refer to actual life experiences which, whether we come to know them reflectively or not, are experiences of the Spirit. It is important that we experience them in the right way. In the case of these indications of the actual experience of the Spirit in the midst of banal everyday life, it can no longer be a question of analyzing them individually right down to their ultimate depth — which is the Spirit. And no attempt can be made to make a systematic tabular summary of such experiences. Only arbitrarily and unsystematically selected examples are possible....

"Let us take, for instance, someone who is dissatisfied with his life, who cannot make the good will, errors, guilt, and fatalities of his life fit together, even when, as often seems impossible, he adds remorse to this accounting. He cannot see how he is to include God as an entry in the accounting, as one that makes the debit and credit, the notional and the actual values, come out right. This person surrenders himself to God or — both more imprecisely and more precisely — to the hope of an incalculable ultimate reconciliation of his existence in which dwells he whom we call God; he releases his unresolved and uncalculated existence, he lets go in trust and hope and does not know how this miracle occurs that he cannot himself enjoy and possess as his own self-actuated possession.

"Here is someone who discovers that he can forgive though he receives no reward for it, and silent forgiveness from the other side is taken as self-evident.

"Here is someone who tries to love God although no response of love seems to come from God's silent incomprehensibility, although no wave of emotive wonder any longer supports him, although he can no longer confuse himself and his life-force with God; although he thinks he will die from such a love because it seems like death and absolute denial; because with such a love one appears to call into the void and the completely ineffable; because this love seems like a ghastly leap into groundless space; because everything seems untenable and apparently meaningless.

"Here is someone who does his duty where it can apparently only be done with the terrible feeling that he is denying himself and doing something ludicrous, for which no one will thank him.

"Here is a person who is really good to someone from whom no echo of understanding and thankfulness is heard in return, whose goodness is not even repaid by the feeling of having been selfless, noble, and so on.

"Here is someone who is silent although he could defend himself, although he is unjustly treated; who keeps silent without feeling that his silence is his sovereign unimpeachability.

"Here is someone who obeys not because he must and would otherwise find it inconvenient to disobey, but purely on account of that mysterious, silent, and incomprehensibility we call God and the will of God.

"Here is a person who renounces something without thanks or recognition and even without a feeling of inner satisfaction.

"Here is someone who is absolutely lonely, who finds all the right elements of life pale shadows; for whom all trustworthy handholds take him into the infinite distance and who does not run away from this loneliness but treats it with ultimate hope.

"Here is someone who discovers that his most acute concepts and most intellectually refined operations of the mind do not fit; that the unity of consciousness and that of which one is conscious in the destruction of all systems is now to be found only in pain; that he cannot resolve the immeasurable multitude of questions and yet cannot keep to the clearly known content of individual experiences and to the sciences.

"Here is someone who suddenly notices how the tiny trickle of his life wanders through the wilderness of the banality of existence, apparently without aim and with the heartfelt fear of complete exhaustion. And yet he hopes, he knows not how, that this trickle will find the infinite expanse of the ocean, even though it may still be covered by the gray sands which seem to extend forever before him.

"One could go on like this forever, perhaps even without coming to that experience which for this or that man is the experience of the Spirit, freedom, and grace in his life. For every man has that experience in accordance with the particular historical and individual situation of his specific life. Every man! But he has, so to speak, to dig it out from under the rubbish of everyday experience and must not run away from it when it begins to become legible, as though it were only an undermining and disturbance of the self-evidence of his everyday life and of his scientific assurance.

"Let me repeat, though I may say it in almost the same words: where the one and entire hope is given beyond all individual hopes, which comprehends all impulses in silent promise,

- where a responsibility in freedom is still accepted and borne where it has no apparent offer of success and advantage,

- where a man experiences and accepts his ultimate freedom which no earthly compulsions can take away from him,

- where the leap into the darkness of death is accepted as the beginning of everlasting promise,

- where the sum of all accounts of life, which no one can calculate alone, is understood by the incomprehensible Other as good, though it still cannot be 'proven,'

- where the fragmentary experience of love, beauty, and joy is experienced and accepted purely and simply as the promise of love, beauty, and joy, without their being understood in ultimate cynical skepticism as a cheap form of consolation for some final deception,

- where the bitter, deceptive, and vanishing everyday world is withstood until the accepted end and accepted out of a force whose ultimate source is still unknown to us but can be tapped by us,

- where one dares to pray into a silent darkness and knows that one is heard, although no answer seems to come back about which one might argue and rationalize,

- where one lets oneself go unconditionally and experiences this capitulation as true victory,

- where falling becomes true uprightness,

- where desperation is accepted and is still secretly accepted as trustworthy without cheap trust,

- where a man entrusts all his knowledge and all his questions to the silent and all-inclusive mystery which is loved more than all our individual knowledge which makes us such small people,

- where we rehearse our own deaths in everyday life and try to live in such a way as we would like to die, peaceful and composed,

- where . . . (as I have said, we could go on and on):

- *there* is God and his liberating grace.

There we find what we Christians call the Holy Spirit of God. Then we experience something which is inescapable (even when suppressed) in life and which is offered to our freedom with the question whether we want to accept it or whether we want to shut ourselves up in a hell of freedom by trying to barricade ourselves against it. There is the mysticism of everyday life, the discovery of God in all things; there is the sober intoxication of the Spirit, of which the Fathers and the liturgy speak, which we cannot reject or despise because it is real. Let us look for that experience in our own lives. Let us seek the specific experiences in which something like that happens to us. If we find them, we have had the experience of the Spirit which we are talking about."[32]

Thus, any person able to die to self in daily life, albeit often in a hidden way, is a mystic of everyday life. The sin unto death, to Rahner, occurs only when a person freely and radically with his or her entire being decides that "this hope that I cannot uproot in my heart is the greatest absurdity."[33]

Rahner gives specific examples of these mystics of everyday life — whom he also calls "unknown saints" — in his brief piece, "Why Become or Remain a Jesuit?" He writes: "I still see around me living in many of my companions a readiness for disinterested service carried out in silence, a readiness for prayer, for abandonment to the incomprehensibility of God, for the calm acceptance of death in whatever form it may come, for total dedication to the following of Christ crucified."[34] He mentions his friend Alfred Delp, who signed his final vows with chained hands and then went to his death in Berlin for anti-Nazi activity. A Jesuit unknown to Indian intellectuals because of his humble work with the poor; a Jesuit student chaplain, beaten by police along with his students, but without the satisfaction of considering himself a revolutionary; a hospital chaplain whose daily work with the sick and dying made even death a "dull routine"; the prison chaplain appreciated more for the cigarettes he brings than for the Gospel he preaches — such people impress Rahner. Thus, his mystic of everyday life, his unknown saint, is the "one who with difficulty and without any clear evidence of success plods away at the task of awakening in just a few men and women a small spark of faith, of hope and of charity."[35] This is the reason the word "courage" so often appears in Rahner's writing. It takes genuine courage to live life in self-emptying love and service of others.

Contrast Experiences

The negative aspect of the mysticism of everyday life also shows itself in the experiences of evil, or powerful experiences of "what ought not to be." For example, why do even atheists or agnostics — who contend that we are nothing more than clever animals produced by evolution and that all life naturally ends in death — vehemently protest against death as something appalling, as life's ultimate meaninglessness? "According to your theory," Rahner says, "death should be something obvious. Why then do you experience it as something shocking, as the ultimate absurdity of existence?"[36] Where do atheists and agnostics acquire their often acute sensitivity to injustice, evil, suffering, and death if not from an even deeper experience of ultimate life, fulfillment, and meaning? In short, what provides the grounding for a radical experience of "what ought not to be" for those who deny ultimate meaning a priori? "They do so," Rahner says, "because deep down and without being aware of it they use a standard by which [these evils] may rightly be considered meaningless and dreadful."[37]

For example, when Albert Camus cries out that heaven is

not worth the death of one innocent child, has he not in fact experienced even more deeply what *ought* to be? If God does not exist, how can anyone have an absolute responsibility toward anyone else? Outrage against Hitler, Stalin, Idi Amin, Pol Pot, the Ayatollah — the mass murderers of our age; the deep conviction that we must not forget Auschwitz, Biafra, Armenia, and Cambodia, that we eventually must give an account of ourselves before the victims — these flow from an absolute commitment to life, truth, conscience, and love.

Only against the ever-present, deeper, often overlooked experience of true life, eternal life, absolute truth, good, meaning, and love do most people poignantly experience suffering, evil, injustice, brutality, misery, and death as something that ought not to be. These negative realities contrast sharply with the positive, universal experience of God rooted in every human heart. Just as white chalk on a blackboard shows up clearly, so life's negative experiences acutely affect people because of the even deeper and more powerful positive experience of God's life, truth, meaning, and love rooted in the heart. Yet this horizon against which all other experiences are contrasted, the horizon of the experience of God, often is taken for granted or overlooked. Again, Rahner asks: "Why is any kind of radical moral cynicism impossible for a person who has ever discovered his real self?...Why does ultimate fidelity not capitulate in the face of death? Why is real moral goodness not afraid of the apparently hopeless futility of all striving?"[38]

Love of Neighbor

Perhaps the paramount contrast experience is loving another human being. Unconditional love of a person who is both finite and sinful is seemingly impossible and absurd. We saw in the previous chapter, however, that love of neighbor *is* love of God. By affirming another's absolute worth — despite finitude and sinfulness — through self-forgetting love, a person experiences the mysticism of everyday life. Unrequited loving; doing good or forgiving another, and having this goodness or forgiveness taken for granted; selflessly loving and forgiving without the compensation of feeling good about one's selflessness; remaining silent rather than striking back in the face of unjust treatment; patiently and mysteriously penetrating one's own and one's beloved's sinfulness and reaching a core of infinite goodness — these are all ways to experience the mysticism of everyday life.

The mysticism of everyday life which engenders a communion of brothers and sisters can occur in the midst of the banality of everyday life. "The launchpad, if we may so call it," Rahner writes, "may be flimsy and narrow, and rise so scarcely above the flat plain of the everyday as to be hardly noticed at all. But these trivialities — the biblical glass of water to someone thirsty, a kind word at someone's sickbed, the refusal to take some small, mean advantage even of someone whose selfishness has infuriated us, or a thousand other everyday trifles — can be the unassuming accomplishment by which the actual attitude of unselfish brotherly and sisterly communion is consummated. And this communion is life's proper deed."[39]

Rahner emphasizes that the human person is social by nature. Thus, if we really believe in the Gospel, how will we treat others and transform society? What is the Church and what should it be doing in this regard? For Rahner, the sociopolitical meaning of the Gospel's injunction to love one's neighbor needs particular emphasis. Genuine love of neighbor must not only be individualistic; it must also reform unjust social structures which harm one's neighbors. As Rahner says, "If Christianity is love of God and love of neighbor, and if in our day love of God can only be realized in a mystical experience of God's nearness, and if love of neighbor can only be realized by attending to a sociopolitical mission, which every person has, . . . then precisely in our day Christianity has a mystical and social component. And especially in our day, because without the mystical component a mere external indoctrination concerning God's existence and Christianity and its content does not suffice. And precisely in our day, a sociopolitical or social component is of special significance, because the contemporary person cannot find credible true love of neighbor, which comes from God and witnesses to God, if it were to limit itself to a merely intimate realm between persons, and not take into account the actual social, sociopolitical, and sociocritical task."[40] In short, the experience of the God of love must sometimes lead to Christian love in the sociopolitical sphere.

Mysticism in Ordinary Dress

In addition to the mysticism of everyday life, Rahner speaks of a "mysticism in ordinary dress," or a "mysticism of the masses."[41] His odd term refers to the spirituality of those in the contemporary charismatic movements. Such people claim to be intoxicated with the Holy Spirit and often experience dramatic faith conversions, speak glossolalia, publicly and loudly proclaim their faith, prophesy, experience swooning or "slaying" in the Spirit, and heal others. Their mysticism occurs more commonly than the extraordinary mysticism of the great saints — and more ostentatiously than the mysticism of everyday life. Although Rahner considers himself to be a "sober" Christian, he takes seriously the various charismatic movements in the Church. Because of their often unusual power to intensify the ever-present experience of God and to deepen the Christian faith, hope, and love of those in such movements, Rahner says that they are a real and concrete expression of Christianity.

He adds that we are not "forced either to recognize expressions of religious enthusiasm, at least when they are genuine, as the unadulterated operation of the Holy Spirit, or to discount them from the start, even from the human point of view, as 'rubbish,' the result of human religious impulses going off the rails."[42] He sometimes chides the tendency of some in the charismatic movements for the often naive and self-conscious way in which they identify every emotional twitch as a sign of the Holy Spirit. However, he would not side with those who reject these phenomena outright as signs of emotional abnormality.

Rahner is cautious when he writes: "It is true that these charismatic experiences do not bring about such a graced-filled awareness of God's presence in entirely pure and clear form, for they can distort the real experience of grace in a new way precisely because they break through the imprisoning objectivity·of everyday religious awareness."[43] Thus, charismatic experiences can both clarify and distort the experience of God.

However, in contrast to bogus phenomena produced either by the devil or by autosuggestion, genuine Christian charismatic gifts can awaken the love of God ever-present in the human heart, intensify it, and make it more explicit in everyday life. Moreover, they make themselves felt precisely within the Christian community as such. They encourage and build up community. They may also make the charismatic person more loving, joyful, peaceful, patient, kind, good, trustworthy, gentle, and self-controlled (Gal. 5:22). In short, the gifts of the Spirit produce the fruits of the Spirit, purify the mysticism of daily life, and make it easier for the one gifted charismatically to love others and to surrender to the holy Mystery that embraces life.

Rahner understands charismatic phenomena as the psychological or parapsychological reverberations of the God-experience throughout a person's psychosomatic structure. They can be understood as experiences of the Holy Spirit expressed in psychosomatic language, or as the God experience "percolated" through the person's psyche. As such, they are a great aid in rendering the experience of God more apparent.

Mysticism in ordinary dress has transformed many Christians by bringing about genuine conversions, imbued them with a taste for prayer, opened their hearts to the mysteries of the Scriptures, and bestowed upon them their first real experience of Christian community. Frequently this mysticism cuts across confessional lines and imparts a deep sense of ecumenism. For Rahner, however, this enthusiastic mysticism in ordinary dress is not the only way to be a contemporary Christian. "These charismatic groups," he writes, "should not feel that they alone are simply the only true and living Christianity.... There is a mysticism of daily life, the finding of God in all things, the *sober* drunkenness of the Spirit mentioned by the Church Fathers and ancient liturgy, which we dare not reject or disdain just because it is *sober.*"[44]

Rahner predicts that Christian spirituality in the future will be of two types which he understands as related to each other but never able to be separated into their chemically pure components. "The one type," Rahner says, "though decidedly Christian, and though those who practice it pray and receive the sacraments, is what I have called a wintry spirituality. It is closely allied with the torment of atheists, though obviously people who practice it are not atheists. The other type is found among the newer enthusiastic or charismatic movements, such as Catholic pentecostalism. In this type of spirituality there is an almost naive immediacy to God, bordering on a naive faith in the power of the Holy Spirit. Whether it is correct or not, well, it remains to be seen."[45] Rahner respects charismatic mysticism, but prefers the wintry type of spirituality, the more "sober" mysticism of daily life, found in courageous perseverance in silent faith, hope, trust, love, and unselfish service, despite life's seeming emptiness.

The Extraordinary Mysticism of the Saints

Rahner's interest in the experience of God permits us to understand his wish to "hear the views of the person who himself experiences most clearly and with the least distortion the relationship which exists between the human subject and the reality we call God."[46] Rahner thus looks to the saints' experiences of God because of their special clarity, intensity, and ability to explain the relationship everyone has with God.

The extraordinary mysticism of the Church's famous saints can teach us much in this increasingly secular and self-sufficient age, an age in which God is seemingly absent. "It is more urgent than ever," Rahner writes, "to have a theology and, even beyond this, an initiation into man's personal experience of God. And the classical masters...are thoroughly good and irreplaceable teachers when it is a question of developing such a theology and mystagogy that makes intelligible the personal experience of God."[47] A theology which awakens people to their own inner depths can illuminate the experience of God not only for Christians but also for those who would even deny God's existence. Moreover, a theology and mystagogy drawn from the experiences of the great Christian mystics would help Christians in their dialogue with Eastern religions.

Because the classical mystics interpreted their experiences of God with the terms of their day, their writings must be transposed for contemporary use. "And such a transposition," Rahner notes, "could be fruitful, because the depth and radicality of the experience of God which the classical authors describe are not so commonplace that we could discover in ourselves the buds and traces of this experience of God just as easily without their help as with it."[48] Since "the characteristic piety of a mystic is given a special depth and power by the specifically mystical element of his piety,"[49] Rahner views the mystic as the one who purifies and amplifies without distortion the often barely audible and distorted experience of God found in everyone. We saw in the previous chapter, for example, the important role the mysticism of St. Ignatius assumed in both Rahner's theology and spiritual life. Thus, one can understand why Rahner finds the contemporary theological lack of interest in mystical questions so disappointing.[50]

To define precisely the specific element or elements in the extraordinary mysticism of the great saints is extremely difficult. Rahner writes, however, that "we do after all possess a vague empirical concept of Christian mysticism: the religious experiences of the saints, all that they experienced of closeness to God, of higher impulses, of visions, inspirations, of the consciousness of being under the special and personal guidance of the Holy Spirit, of ecstasies, etc. All this is comprised in our understanding of the word mysticism without our having to stop here to ask what exactly it is that is of ultimate importance in all this, and in what this proper element consists."[51] Thus, the mysticism of the great saints has something to do with their enhanced God consciousness, their raptures, their visions, and their special sensitivity to the least motion of the Holy Spirit operative within them.

Yet he also insists that "in *every* human person (from the essence of spirit and from the always offered grace of God's self-communication to each person) there is something like an anonymous, unthematic, perhaps repressed, basic experience of being oriented to God, which is constitutive of the human person in his basic make-up (of nature and grace), which can be repressed but not destroyed, which is 'mystical' or (if you prefer a more cautious terminology) has its climax in what the classical masters called infused contemplation."[52]

Two things should be noted. First, Rahner seemingly agrees with those early Church Fathers who did not differentiate sharply between seemingly weak experiences of God and the extraordinary mysticism of the saints. Second, he tentatively accepts "infused contemplation" as the central phenomenon in Christian mysticism—not ecstasies, visions, and other such extraordinary phenomena commonly associated with mysticism. On the other hand, Rahner does not agree with theologians who distinguish too sharply between infused contemplation and such phenomena.

The classical masters describe infused contemplation as an experience of God's love that penetrates, dominates, and controls the soul's innermost core. The mystic no longer reaches out for God but is instead gripped firmly by God — surrendering in faith, hope, and love is the mystic's only act. Infused contemplation also bestows upon the person a vague, obscure, dark, yet rich and satisfying loving-knowledge of God. The mystic is absolutely certain that God and God alone is acting. The total inability to awaken, prolong, renew, to describe adequately, or to foresee the beginning or the end of these experiences likewise characterizes infused contemplation.

One can see the influence of an older tradition on Rahner when he states that the term "mysticism" can mean both "an experience, the interior meeting and union of a man with the divine infinity that sustains him and all other being...as well as the attempt to give a systematic exposition of this experience, or reflection upon it (hence a scientific 'discipline')."[53] Thus, mysticism can refer either to the experience or to the theology, the systematic explanation of the experience.

Moreover, in Christian mysticism, this divine infinity is nothing less than the *personal,* albeit incomprehensible, God. Rahner insists, too, that "the mystic experiences the influence from the Absolute as that which is most inward in his own soul...as the submerging of the soul in its source...[and] always as a gift."[54]

Yet Rahner is wary of the term "infused contemplation" because it connotes God's extrinsic and sporadic influx into the soul, an influx that is God's *special* grace to an elite. He understands that both the mysticism of everyday life and the extraordinary mysticism of the saints occur in the "normal" realm of grace and faith. For him, therefore, the extraordinary mysticism of the saints "is not specifically different from the ordinary life of grace (as such)....Any other theory of Christian mysticism would undoubtedly be either gnosticism or theosophy and either an overestimation of mysticism or else a *fundamental underestimation of the real depth of the 'ordinary' Christian life of grace.*"[55]

To Rahner, "mystical experience must not be interpreted as something which fundamentally transcends and supersedes the supernatural experience of the Spirit in faith. That is why the 'specific difference' of such experience, as distinct from the Christian's 'normal' experience of the Spirit, must belong to man's *'natural'* sphere.... *Psychologically* mystical experiences differ from normal everyday occurrences in consciousness only in the natural sphere and to that extent are fundamentally learnable."[56] Even the "normal" Christian in certain circumstances, to Rahner, could learn meditative and contemplative techniques — those psychosomatic techniques which would enable him or her to sink more deeply into self to experience God in a purer, more intense, and clearer form.

Thus, the extraordinary mysticism of the saints differs from the everyday mysticism of "normal" Christians, but not because the former is a "higher" form of the experience of God. "They are different," Rahner writes, "because their natural substratum (for example, an experience of the suspension of the faculties) is as such different from the psychological circumstances of everyday life."[57] To put it more concretely, the specific way in which the great saints experience God belongs to the person's natural ability for concentration, contemplation, meditation, submersion into the self, self-emptying, and other psychomental techniques often associated with Eastern mysticisms.[58]

The mysticism of the great saints, therefore, results from an unusual — though natural — psychological way of experiencing God in faith, hope, and love. "Meditation and similar spiritual 'exercises' are not thereby deprecated," Rahner writes. "For example, feeding the hungry, giving drink to the thirsty, clothing the naked, and the like — though natural acts in themselves — can be of extreme significance for salvation."[59] The same can be said of natural meditative, contemplative, and other psychomental techniques which help root faith, hope, and love more deeply in the person's core.

Rahner appreciates these contemplative techniques as "rehearsals, so to speak, for admitting and accepting in radical freedom fundamental experiences of the Spirit whenever they occur in life. These exercises can *also* (but not solely) be the point at which such experiences of the Spirit become clearer and more explicit and are grasped by man's ultimate basic freedom in such a way that they amount to a decision embracing the whole of existence and leading to salvation."[60] Because such techniques intensify the primordial experience of God rooted in every human heart, perhaps one should speak of the "awakened contemplation" of the saints instead of their "infused contemplation."

Rahner thus rejects any elitist interpretation of life "which can see man's perfection only in the trained mystic."[61] He insists that the New Testament "awards to all who love their neighbor unselfishly and therein experience God that final salvation in God's judgment which is not surpassed even by the highest ascent or the deepest absorption of the mystic."[62]

Conclusion

The mysticism of everyday life is nothing else than the "more excellent way" of love described by St. Paul in 1 Corinthians 13: "Love is patient and kind; love is not jealous or boastful; it is not arrogant or rude. Love does not insist on its own way; it is not irritable or resentful; it does not rejoice at wrong, but rejoices in the right. Love bears all things, believes all things, endures all things" (1 Cor. 13:4–7). Paul prefers love to the charismatic gifts, although he wants all Christians to desire the charismatic gifts. The Church canonized the saints — not for their mysticism, but for their heroic love.

Love must be the norm against which everything is measured. For example, some contemporary Christians often give the impression that there is only one way to be a Christian. Speaking in tongues, charismatic healings, academic theology, the pope, peace and justice, political and liberation theology, preferential option for the poor, the women's movements, Christian pacifism, mysticism, appearances of Our Lady at Medjugorje,[63] and the like are often touted as the more excellent way. But as St. Paul says, without love — *the* mysticism of everyday life — they are nothing. They may catalyze a more intense Christian life, but they may also be fads, ideologies, and idols. No Christian need feel obliged to be present at all the rallies, even when they are genuine.

Rahner's theology of the mysticism of everyday life challenges everyone to look more closely at what is actually going on in the depths of their daily lives. What is implicit, hidden, anonymous, repressed, or bursting forth from the center of all we do? To Rahner, there is nothing profane about the depths of ordinary life. Whenever there is a radical self-surrender, an absolute yielding of everything, a surrender to the mystery that embraces all life — there is the Spirit of the crucified and risen Christ, the mysticism of everyday life.

Notes

1. "Christian Living Formerly and Today," *TI VII*, 13.

2. Ibid., 14.

3. Ibid., 15.

4. *Faith in a Wintry Season*, 115.

5. "Christian Living Formerly and Today," *TI VII*, 15. Also see *Karl Rahner in Dialogue*, 176.

6. For example, see *Handbuch der Pastoraltheologie*, 2d ed. (Freiburg im Breisgau: Herder, 1972), 3:523.

7. *Faith in a Wintry Season*, 115.

8. *Karl Rahner in Dialogue*, 182.

9. "Mysticism," *Encyclopedia of Theology* (New York: Seabury Press, 1975), 1010–11.

10. "Reflections on the Problem of the Gradual Ascent to Christian Perfection," *TI III*, 23.

11. "Eternity from Time," *TI XIX*, 169–77.

12. Ibid., 177.

13. "Everyday Things," *Belief Today*, trans. Ray and Rosaleen Ockenden (New York: Sheed and Ward, 1967), 20–21.

14. Ibid., 32–33.

15. This is a constant theme in Rahner's *Biblical Homilies*, trans. Desmond Forristal and Richard Strachan (New York: Herder and Herder, 1966).

16. "On the Theology of Worship," *TI XIX*, 147. My emphasis.

17. "The Ignatian Mysticism of Joy in the World," *TI III*, 291. Rahner's emphasis.

18. *Faith in a Wintry Season*, 163.

19. "Experiencing the Spirit," *The Practice of Faith: A Handbook of Contemporary Spirituality*, ed. Karl Lehmann and Albert Raffelt (New York: Crossroad Publishing Co., 1983), 81. Henceforth referred to as *The Practice of Faith*.

20. "The Ignatian Mysticism of Joy in the World," *TI III*, 277–93.

21. Ibid., 293.

22. *Karl Rahner — I Remember*, 84.

23. *Is Christian Life Possible Today?* trans. Salvator Attanasio (Denville, N.J.: Dimension, 1984), 126.

24. "Experiencing the Spirit," *The Practice of Faith*, 81.

25. "Reflections on the Experience of Grace," *TI III*, 86–87. Also see "Experience of Transcendence from the Standpoint of Christian Dogmatics," *TI XVIII*, 173–88.

26. *Karl Rahner in Dialogue*, 152. My emphasis.

27. Karl Rahner, ed., *The Teachings of the Catholic Church* (New York: Alba House, 1966), 99, no. 156. My emphasis.

28. "God of My Daily Routine," *Encounters with Silence*, trans. James M. Demske, S.J. (Westminster, Md.: Newman, 1966), 49.

29. *Biblical Homilies*, 77.

30. "Experiencing the Spirit," *The Practice of Faith*, 81. Also see *Karl Rahner in Dialogue*, 57, 83, 142, 183, 227, 245, and 293; "Reflections on the Experience of Grace," *TI III*, 86–90. "Experience of the Holy Spirit," *TI XVIII*, 189–210.

31. "Experiencing the Spirit," *The Practice of Faith*, 81.

32. Ibid., 81–84.

33. *Karl Rahner in Dialogue*, 291.

34. *Madonna* (Jesuit publication, Melbourne, Australia) (April 1987), 11.

35. Ibid.

36. *Karl Rahner in Dialogue*, 89.

37. Ibid., 90.

38. *Foundations of Christian Faith*, 438.

39. *The Love of Jesus and the Love of Neighbor*, trans. Robert Barr (New York: Crossroad Publishing Co., 1983), 103.

40. *Karl Rahner in Dialogue*, 185.

41. "Religious Enthusiasm and the Experience of Grace," *TI XVI*, 35–51.

42. Ibid., 47–48.

43. Ibid., 46.

44. *Karl Rahner in Dialogue*, 329, 297. My emphasis.

45. *Faith in a Wintry Season*, 35.

46. "Mystical Experience and Mystical Theology," *TI XVII*, 92.

47. "Teresa of Avila: Doctor of the Church," *The Great Church Year*, 362.

48. Ibid., 362–63.

49. See "The Ignatian Mysticism of Joy in the World," *TI III*, 280–81.

50. "Mystical Experience and Mystical Theology," *TI XVII*, 91.

51. "The Ignatian Mysticism of Joy in the World," *TI III*, 279–80.

52. "Teresa of Avila: Doctor of the Church," *The Great Church Year*, 362.

53. *Dictionary of Theology*, 325.

54. Ibid., 325–26.

55. "Mysticism," *Encyclopedia of Theology*, 1010–11. My emphasis.

56. "Mystical Experience and Mystical Theology," *TI XVII*, 95.

57. Ibid., 97–98.

58. Klaus P. Fischer, *Der Mensch als Geheimnis* (Freiburg im Breisgau: Herder, 1974), "Brief von P. Karl Rahner," 406.

59. Ibid., 406.

60. "Experience of the Holy Spirit," *TI XVIII*, 207.

61. "Experience of Transcendence," *TI XVIII*, 175.

62. "Experience of the Holy Spirit," *TI XVIII*, 208.

63. In those rare cases in which the Church proclaims in favor of an appearance of Our Lady, the Church states that one *may* believe this with a *human* faith. It can be asked: Does our Lady ever say anything more than one can find already in Scripture and its living out in the Church's tradition? See Rahner's *Vision and Prophecies* for a thorough treatment of this issue.

Chapter 4

Karl Rahner — Teacher of Prayer

Explicit prayer and penetrating reflection on prayer punctuated Rahner's entire life. When only twenty years old, Rahner published his first article, "Why We Need to Pray,"[1] and on his eightieth birthday he received a copy of the first edition of his new book *Prayers for a Lifetime*.[2] His unexpected death on March 30, 1984, rendered the sickbed composition "Prayer for the Reunion of All Christians" his final text.[3]

For all practical purposes Rahner's first popular books were on prayer, namely, *Encounters with Silence*[4] and *The Need and the Blessing of Prayer*.[5] One commentator describes these books as "certainly typical and vintage Rahner. I wonder, though, whether their mood might not be a bit heavy — even lugubrious — for today's readers. Written shortly after World War II, they intensely reflect the mood of misery of those tragic years."[6] These prayers are indeed vintage Rahner. However, I do not share our commentator's second view because these books were my first encounters with Rahner's writing when I was a Jesuit novice. These books I used and still use for prayer. I also personally know people from many walks of life whose lives were profoundly changed by reading and praying these books. One example: a friend who worked in a halfway house for troubled teenagers found her copy of *Encounters* in the hands of an unwed teenage mother who exclaimed: "Who is this person? He prays just like me!"

Rahner was never one to wear his heart on his sleeve. But he did not hesitate to pray publicly. In fact, he often prayed the rosary while his lectures were being read to American audiences by an interpreter. He enjoyed relating how he and

Cardinal Ottaviani — the same cardinal responsible for a Vatican slap on Rahner's wrist — once prayed the rosary and the litany of Loreto while traveling together. That a senile St. Albert the Great could do nothing more at the end of his distinguished theological life than pray the Hail Mary still impressed Rahner as a great blessing. He hailed the custom of assigning old Jesuits the task of praying for the Society of Jesus, the "work" found after their names in the Jesuit catalogue.[7] When challenged by an interviewer because of his great faith despite the horrors of Nazism, Rahner said: "I believe because I pray."[8] Moreover, "one can rightly answer that at least some of these unfortunate human beings went to the gas chambers praying and believing in God."[9]

Much of Rahner's theology flows out of and then leads back into encounters with the saving, silent presence of the mystery of God's love for us in the crucified and risen Christ, *and* does so without dissolving theology's necessarily critical and rational function. To some extent, one can view Rahner's theology as prayer seeking understanding, as kneeling with the mind before holy Mystery with Christ in the Spirit. Thus Rahner stands in a long line of great Christian theologians who were likewise great teachers of prayer.

The Person as *Homo Orans*

Rahner highlights prayer as the fundamental act of human existence, the act that embraces the entire person — the great religious act. He also views the human person as essentially one called to pray, *homo orans.* To Rahner, to pray is to *be* in the most profound sense possible. He sees Christ's humanity as prayer's perfect paradigm: total, unconditional surrender to holy Mystery. Likewise, he considers the God-question and the prayer-question as two sides of the same coin. Prayer, to Rahner, is "the last moment of speech before the silence; the act of self surrender just before the incomprehensible God disposes of one; the reflection immediately preceding the act of letting oneself fall — after the last of one's own efforts — and full of trust — into the infinite fullness and silence that reflection can never grasp."[10]

The God who communicates his very own self to us, not an abstract God, stands at the center of Rahner's theology of prayer — in fact, his entire theology. Life's secret ingredient is the grasp of God's silent incomprehensibility before which we can only fall dumb in adoration; before which and toward which we exist, whether we wish to or not.[11]

Through God's self-communication, we actually experience God-above-us (holy Mystery), God-with-us (enfleshed Word), and God-in-us (Holy Spirit). Because we are made for the fullness of the infinite Mystery, we are never totally fulfilled by the finite, by anything in this world. Because we are historical and body-persons, we are always in search of that one person who will totally fulfill us — whom Rahner calls the "absolute savior," the crucified and risen Word. Because we are also beings of interiority, our immense longing draws us into the deepest levels of self wherein dwells the Holy Spirit. We are essentially *ec*static beings drawn to God's holy mystery, worldly and historical beings attracted to the absolute savior, and *en*static beings drawn to our deepest interior by the fontal fullness of the Spirit of love. In short, we are called to be and to live trinitarian prayer. This grounds Rahner's view of the human person as *homo orans,* as one called to be a living pray-er.

Prayer to the Personal God

Rahner insists that prayer is a gift, a grace, a response to something previously put on our lips. Even the desire to pray is God's gift and also prayer. Although wholly God's gift, it is also the person's free act. Paradoxically, Rahner says that there is nothing in prayer we can claim for ourselves and yet we do freely respond to (or reject) this gift.[12]

The early Christians, in Rahner's view, took over from Jesus absolute confidence in the goodness and power of his heavenly Father. Jesus taught them that they would indeed be heard, if they prayed in his name. All prayer for Rahner is made in Jesus' name, though often only implicitly. Jesus had also taught them to expect his return. The early Christians prayed with great fervor, "Maranatha — Our Lord, come!" In time, however, Christian prayer freed itself from past and future to sink tranquilly into itself. The lingering look at the mysteries of Christ's life, death, and resurrection replaced the prayer of urgent expectation. This turn away from the future and also the tendency to spiritualize prayer, to turn it into "pure" prayer occurring only at the soul's still point — Rahner does not judge this as all to the good of Christian spirituality.

Genuine Christian prayer should impart both a deep confidence in God's love as manifested in Christ and a profound sense of sinfulness, of always falling short. Rahner claims that the more God-given gifts the saints received, the better they saw their own sinfulness and poverty. "Lord, I am not worthy" is a prayer also for the perfect.

Because of the human person's social nature, all Christian prayer — no matter how private it may seem — relies on the community which it serves. The Christian always prays in the name of Christ and of the Church no matter how implicit that awareness may be. The *ultimate* meaning of community liturgical prayer, to Rahner, is to lead the individual to God as a member of the people of God.

Rahner stresses the interpersonal dialogic quality of Christian prayer. To him, God is far more than the ground of being. "For me," Rahner writes, "the truly incomprehensible reality is to be found less in the fact that such an immense and primordial reality which is behind me, under me, above me, permeating all reality exists, and more in the fact that I can say to this reality: 'Our Father in heaven, hallowed be Thy name.' And I would like to add right away: I can only believe that this is possible if I trust that God himself has taken this initiative — God as the Absolute who accomplishes becoming so small that God even has become human. But why do I trust that God can do such a miracle? Because I build on the fact that he is greater than, but can become smaller than, all my metaphysical concepts of him, and because I have had the experience that such arrogance on the part of the tiny creature 'delights' the Absolute. That is, I pray, and I have the impression that my prayer reaches God."[13]

The most important aspect of human dignity, to Rahner, is that "man can at all events speak to God, address him and in address come to him...in grace as the place of prayer, which is everywhere.... The creature is a genuine, true reality who does not evaporate into nothingness when he faces God."[14] Saying yes to God with one's entire being, with the help of God's grace, actuates a person's "highest possibility."[15]

Despite Rahner's respect for the graced experience of God found in Eastern religions, he criticizes their interpretation of it as impersonal or as a dissolution into the Absolute. He rejects quickly any spirituality which tends to obscure or to dissolve the interpersonal, dialogic relationship between God and the person. Taking his cue from the Scriptures, Rahner insists that such a dissolution makes genuine praise and worship of God impossible. One seriously misunderstands Rahner's view of God as mystery if one does not understand God as the loving, personal incomprehensibility.

However, Rahner does not defend prayer as dialogue with God naively. In the I-Thou relationship between the person and God, "God's most original word to us in our free uniqueness is not a word arising momentarily...but is we ourselves as integral, total entities and in our reference to the incomprehensible mystery we call God.... When a person, in the Spirit and by grace, experiences himself as the one spoken by God to himself and understands this as his true [graced] essence...and when he admits this existence and freely accepts it in prayer as the word of God in which God promises himself to man with his Word, his prayer is already...dialogic, an exchange with God. Then the person hears himself as God's address...as the self-promised word in which God sets up a listener and to which he speaks himself as an answer."[16] In short, in prayer God speaks *us to ourselves.*

The Prayer of Petition

Rahner notes that some contemporary Christians regard the prayer of petition as a primitive and outdated way of praying. They assert that one should worship and praise God and not ask for either heavenly or earthly things. However, the Scriptures and the great saints used and taught the prayer of petition. The prayer Jesus used and taught his own disciplines, the Our Father, is essentially a prayer of petition.

If God is immutable, how can petitionary prayer be meaningful? The incarnation means, to Rahner, that the Word *became* flesh. The eternally unchangeable Word became man. Thus, God who is above all change has a real history in the life, death, and resurrection of Jesus Christ. "God can become something,"

Rahner writes. "He who is unchangeable in himself can himself become subject to change in something else."[17] Christians, therefore, must accept not only the mystery of the one triune God but also the mystery of the immutable God changing and having a real history in Jesus' human reality. Thus, God experienced all of human life and is personally involved in and concerned with our lives. This is the theological foundation for the prayer of petition.

The prayer of petition fascinates Rahner because this is the prayer through which a person brings the self as a whole — yet in all particular aspects of his or her life — before God. This prayer has the special power to remind us of our humanity, that we are indeed spirit-in-world, that our prayer must penetrate all life. The person who prays in this way comes before God as a person of everyday, banal, and often humdrum needs — just as he or she really is and is really willed by God to be. All prayer, in fact, must be an acceptance of the fact that we were created.

"There is a prayer of petition," Rahner writes, "which speaks to God and ... boldly and explicitly ventures to ask him for bread, peace, restraint of ... enemies, health ... and a host of such earthly and highly problematic things. That such a prayer combines a great measure of 'self-will' (for one presents to Him one's own desires) with a supreme degree of submissiveness (for one prays to Him whom one cannot compel, persuade or charm, but only beg), that here there is a mingling and an incomprehensible fusion of the greatest boldness with the deepest humility, of life with death, this makes the prayer of petition in one respect not the lowest but the highest, the most divinely human form of prayer."[18] One affirms oneself, yet surrenders wholly to God and thus adores him.

Genuine prayer of petition is not a "pestering" of God because a person opens his or her heart to God's incomprehensible love "in which alone one is always heard. Only that petition which is truly sure of being heard is petitionary prayer at all."[19] One does not pester God simply because one prays for something specific. Still, one who prays in this way must have an attitude of absolute surrender to God's incomprehensible freedom. "When," Rahner writes, "a person places himself before God as one who as a threatened creature totally submits to God and at the same time wills a particular thing unquestioningly and legitimately, when he is one delivering himself up in his concreteness to God, then he is uttering a prayer of petition.... When petitionary prayer is understood in this way, the question of how it is granted (if it is granted) is of secondary importance."[20]

On the basis of Scripture and the long history of Christianity, Rahner knows that the prayer of petition is always heard. Because of the I-Thou relationship between the human person and God, the person must always surrender lovingly his or her actual everyday self to God. This is the basis of the prayer of petition.

The Prayer of Everyday Life

Perhaps for that reason Rahner exhorts people to "pray in the everyday." As he says, "everything depends on *how* we bear the everyday. It can make us humdrum. However, it can also make us free from ourselves as nothing else can. If we accomplished this freedom and selflessness, then this love, which arises by itself, would soar through all things, directly through the heart of things, would soar out into the infinite expanses of God in longing and holy desire and also take along all the lost things of the everyday as a song of praise of the divine splendor. Our cross of the everyday — on which alone our self-seeking can completely die because it has to be crucified inconspicuously, if it is supposed to die — would become the rising of our love because it would arise from the grave of our own I. And if everything in the everyday becomes such dying, everything in the everyday becomes the rising of love. Then the entire everyday becomes the breathing of love, breathing of longing, of loyalty, of faith, of readiness, of devotion to God, the everyday really becomes itself, wordless prayer! It will remain what it was: difficult, without rhetoric, everyday, inconspicuous. It must be so. Only in this way does it serve the love of God, for only so does it take us away from ourselves. But if we let ourselves be taken by the everyday, our longing, our self-assertion, our obstinacy, our walled-in-selfishness, i.e., if we don't become bitter in our bitterness, ordinary in our ordinariness, everyday in our everydayness, disappointed in our disappointment, if we let ourselves be educated through the everyday to kindness, to patience, to peace and understanding, to forbearance and meekness, to forgiveness and endurance, to selfless loyalty, then the everyday is no longer the everyday, then it is prayer. Then all diversity becomes one in the love of God, all effusion remains collected in God, all exteriority remains in God inwardly. Then all going out into the world, the everyday, becomes a going into God's unity, which is eternal life."[21]

In order to pray the everyday properly, however, one must take up "regular prayer which is practiced without regard to the desire and mood of the moment,...[for instance], prayer at the ringing of the Angelus, the rosary by oneself or with one's family, the silent private visit to a church and the tabernacle outside of the times of common divine service, and other devout practices of old customs as, for example, showing respect while passing a church or an image of the cross, making the sign of the cross while slicing a loaf of bread, the sign of the cross which a child requests and receives from its parents in the evening."[22] Thus, in order that everyday life be in fact a prayer, one must also pray at specific times and have specific devotions.

In the following letter to a young man who experienced difficulty praying, Rahner offered this advice: "Dear Gunther: Actually what you write about yourself and your prayer life is wonderful and not at all so awful as to call for the harsh sentence that you pass on yourself and your prayer. You do pray. Whether it be an Our Father or a long prayer, the difference is not so important. Even if one simply says, 'Dear God, help me!' that is already splendid. In so doing, one does not need to know exactly how God will help when everything is going quite well. And if the actual prayer is preceded by a prolonged period of reflection during which you are concerned with yourself, then what actually happens is only what the masters of the spiritual life recommend for meditation. First one thinks about God, one's own obligations, tasks, cares, and needs. Then this reflection slowly ripens into real prayer. With all that I'm not saying that you cannot learn to pray better, which you indeed can and must. As long as one's life has not yet flowed into the face-to-face, eternal praise of God — no one has already succeeded in prayer in its utmost and perfect form. In this we are always beginners.

"There are many methods by which one can slowly learn

to pray better because prayer — however much it is God's grace and gift — presupposes human psychology which must be taken into consideration if one really wants to pray. Just as in other spiritual matters one must slowly learn to concentrate, to intensify one's awareness of such realities, so too is it with 'recollection' in prayer. On the one hand, one must gain a real distance from the superficialities of one's life, and, on the other hand, still learn to take this multiplicity of thoughts, tasks, cares, disappointments, joys, and the like, to God and in a certain sense to 're-collect' them there.

"In addition, there are many 'tricks' (in the good sense) for easier and better prayer. St. Ignatius of Loyola's *Spiritual Exercises* enumerates them. Read it for yourself! Try sometimes to linger reflectively on the individual words of a prayer you know by heart — to clarify, to unfold for yourself the content of these words. Such meditative reflection should naturally flow into a real prayer to God. As crazy as this may sound in our day, I would still recommend that you sometimes try to pray the rosary by yourself, alone. The calm, peaceful, vocal repetition of the same words and attention to the invoked mysteries of Jesus' life therein can evoke that real silence in which one lingers in God's presence — if in so doing one doesn't grow impatient but slowly tries to practice a little.

"After all, spiritual directors know full well that genuine prayer does not ultimately depend upon a profusion of thoughts brought before the loving God — in the final analysis not even upon the various petitions and wishes with which one attempts to some extent to preoccupy God (even if prayer is tremendously important for us and not really for God). Rather it ultimately depends upon a recollected silence (may one even say emptiness?) in which the whole person confidently and lovingly entrusts himself or herself to God's silent mystery. Just as one ultimately cannot learn to ski through theoretical lectures, but must ski in order to learn to ski — just as in skiing one must again and again start from scratch, even if one in the beginning falls and must always pick oneself up again — so too is it with prayer. One can learn prayer only by praying.

"Your letter indicates clearly that you pray. Do not give it up. Always begin again. You've begun and with patience you will always learn to pray better. When one interprets — repeatedly and correctly — the again and again new experiences of one's life, then these new experiences always give rise to a new, hitherto unknown way to walk prayerfully before God. To bring what is new in one's life before God, regardless of whether it consists of happy or terrible experiences, palpable blessings or even bitter disappointments about oneself — in this way then can everything in one's life really become prayer. By praying one learns to pray."[23]

The Dark Night of Prayer

Anyone who prays faithfully will eventually experience short or long periods of dryness during which one may feel justifiably abandoned by God, or that one has abandoned God. Rahner knows that often one may try to love God, to pray, but no answer comes. The heart is left empty, devoid of all emotion and meaning. Perhaps for the first time one has not confused the life force or the self with God, but still surrenders to the mysterious darkness. This, to Rahner, is excellent prayer, a prayer in which a person repeats Jesus' own prayer on the cross: "My God, my God, why have you forsaken me?" Hence, one's heart of hearts does pray and experiences the "wilderness" of the ever-greater God.

Addressing a German congregation that had experienced the ravages of war, Rahner offers the following advice to those who pray with "rubbled-over" hearts. It requires no commentary. He says: "First, let's say something quite simple about prayer, something very self-evident which is at the very beginning of prayer and which we usually overlook: in prayer we *open* our hearts to God. In order to understand that, to understand it with the heart and not just with the head, two things have to be discussed: the rubbled-over heart and the opening of the heart. . . .

"Do you remember the nights in the cellar, the nights of deadly loneliness amidst the harrowing crush of people? The nights of helplessness and of waiting for a senseless death? The nights when the lights went out, when horror and impotence gripped one's heart, when one mimed being courageous and unaffected? When one's innocently bold and brave words sounded so strangely wooden and empty, as if they were already dead before they even reached the other person? When one finally gave up, when one became silent, when one only waited hopelessly for the end, death? Alone, powerless, empty. And if the cellar really became buried by rubble, then the picture of today's man is complete. For such are we people of today, even if we already have crawled out of the rubbled-over cellars, even if our everyday has already begun again, even if one attempts to assume again the pose of the courageous and vivacious one (oh, how fundamentally strange this pose is, this role which we want to play for ourselves and others). We men of today are still the rubbled-over because as such we have already entered into an exterior destiny, because the exterior destiny — by God, it is so even if it sounds so fantastic and romantic — is only the shadow of events which have occurred in the depths of men: that their hearts are rubbled-over....

"Is the case of the rubbled-over heart hopeless? Is the danger of collapse and being rubbled-over inescapable in the interior man? What can man do if he is supposed to get out of the dungeon of his disguised cold despair and disappointment? How does the opening of one's heart take place? We can say it with one word: by prayer to God and only by prayer. However, precisely because we want to understand what prayer actually is, we have to speak slowly and cautiously. And ask what man has to do when he finds himself in the situation of the rubbled-over heart. This is the first thing: he must stand firm and submit to it.

"You see, when you stand firm and don't flee despair, nor in despairing of your former gods — the vital or the intellectual, the beautiful and the respectable, oh, yes, that they are — which you called God, if you don't despair in the true God, if you stand firm — oh, that is already a miracle of grace which shall be bestowed on you — then you suddenly will become aware that in truth you are not at all rubbled-over, that your jail is closed only to empty finiteness, that its deadly emptiness is only the false appearance of God, that his silence, the eerie stillness, is filled by the Word without words, by Him who is above all names, by Him who is everything in everything. And His silence tells you that He is there....

"And that is the second thing that you should do in your despair: notice that He is there, know that He is with you. Become aware that He has been expecting you for quite some time in the deepest dungeon of your rubbled-over heart. Become aware that He has been quietly listening for a long time. . . .

"And then the third and fourth things come by themselves. Then tranquillity comes by itself. Stillness which no longer goes away. Trust which no longer fears. Security which no longer needs assurance. Power which is mighty in impotence. Life which unfolds into death. Then nothing more is in us than He and the faith which is sheerly imperceptible but fills everything and conquers everything and holds everything fast, that He is, is there, and we are his. And then tranquillity of heart is found. . . .

"And then our heart begins to speak as if by itself. Quietly and without many words. And then it speaks to God who is in us, who holds us although we are falling, who strengthens us although we are weak, who is near to us although we cannot touch Him. Our heart speaks to Him."[24]

Contemplative Religious Orders

Every Christian life, to Rahner, must involve love of neighbor and God. Every Christian must also work, enjoy life, pray, endure life's pains and sorrows, and eventually die.[25] Every Christian is called to do penance and to atone for sins. Thus every Christian life must maintain a dialectical stance between "flight from the world" and "assent to the world." Yet no one Christian can exhaust all the possibilities, tasks, and graces of Christianity. The fullness of Christian life is found in the Church whose members contribute in their unique way to the Church's overall Christian life. Because the Church is a historical organism, the Spirit gives rise to new forms of Christian living within the Church. This is the context in which Rahner speaks about contemplative religious Orders.

Given the Church's history and practice, it is self-evident that there must be contemplative Orders in the Church and that the Church views contemplative life as both legitimate and meaningful. The Second Vatican Council speaks about a certain preeminence of the contemplative Orders and encourages their growth, despite the needs of the so-called active apostolate. Of course, certain concrete forms of expressing this life will die out. To Rahner, for example, the life style of the "stylites," or pillar ascetics, who spent most of their lives atop a column, is no longer fitting — not because the courage for heroic penance no longer exists — but because other aspects of Christian living must be expressed in the contemporary world.

The contemplative Orders, to Rahner, have an important counter-cultural function. "Living in contradiction to the spirit of an age," Rahner writes, "is in truth frequently the most modern and indispensable service a person can do for his or her age."[26] Rahner finds it ironic that contemporary society takes as self-evident a constantly increasing division of labor, praises the protest of hippies, novelists, and musicians against contemporary bourgeois comfort and prosperity, and yet dismisses the contemplative life as worthless. "And in the Church," he writes, "where God cannot and should not be reduced to the human, in this Church should there be no individuals allowed who have made this one (not sole, but irreplaceable) Church vocation the main activity of their lives in the Church and for others?"[27] "In our age," Rahner continues, "witness must be given that God, prayer, renunciation, self-denial...are not simply empty ciphers which a profane humanism should obfuscate and eventually abolish but rather realities without which even love of neighbor cannot last in the long run; without these things it too would lose its radical and eternal validity."[28] The Church needs contemplative Orders whose lives of renunciation and whose worship of God give powerful counter-cultural witness to the ultimate foundation of all human love: God's love.

Rahner views the contemplative life as a real God-given calling, a charism, and not as a refuge for the weak who fear life in the world. People called to this life should have the aptitude and the inclination for solitude, silence, prayer, and genuine contemplation; they must understand that contemplation is their apostolate for the Church. "Action may sometimes be prayer," Rahner explains, "but prayer is also action."[29]

Moreover, a respectful maintaining of separation from the world, to Rahner, never occurs in a pure form. Contemplatives, too, are called not only to pray but also to love the members of their Order, and through their prayer to love the entire Church and world. They "must know that all organized, institutionalized renunciation is only practice for *that* renunciation and *that* death which is the lot of *every* Christian life."[30]

No Christian — not even a contemplative — can be an absolute ascetic. The contemplative remains a human being who may and should enjoy a good meal, deep spiritual friendships — even with members of the opposite sex — and other earthly, human goods.[31] Rahner understands the contemplative life (including the vowed life of poverty, chastity, and obedience in general) to have a special symbolic power because it makes explicit the baptismal vows taken by all Christians. Every Christian is baptized into Christ's death, must love God and neighbor unconditionally, and must live in such a way that her life would be absurd if God did not exist. To Rahner, contemplatives (and other vowed Christians) remind all Christians — and even non-Christians — that we have here no lasting city, that we must all die in Christ to eternal life. However, Christians living a normal human life remind contemplatives (and other vowed Christians) that we are spirit-in-*world*, that the Word became *flesh* and lived a fully human life. "The life of Christians in the world," Rahner writes, "has a message for those who live under the evangelical counsels [poverty, chastity, and obedience]. It tells them that their actions, too, do not compel grace, but rather that grace is bestowed upon those actions. The life of the evangelical counsels has a message for Christians 'in the world.' It tells them that they too are pilgrims, to whom grace comes from above and not *as a result* of their worldly activities (even though it does come *in* those activities)."[32]

Devotional Prayer

Rahner — whose very name is often associated with highly speculative theology — spoke fondly of his devotional works: "Might I say that I regard my devotional works, *The Eternal Year, Encounters with Silence, The Need and the Blessing of Prayer, Spiritual Exercises,* and many similar works not as a secondary by-product of a theology that is sort of an art for art's sake, but at least as important as my specifically theological works. I believe that in some chapters of *The Need and the Blessing of Prayer* there is at least as much theology tucked in — painstaking, thoughtful theology — as in my so-called scholarly or scientific works."[33] When an interviewer marveled at the great range of Rahner's publications and wondered "whether theological creativity isn't a form of prayer and worship for you," Rahner replied: "I at least hope it is."[34]

"Beware the person of no devotions and the person who doesn't pray," Rahner once said to me. After a seminar during which a young scholar argued that we should stop praying because our inadequate theology seems to turn God into an idol, Rahner replied that if we waited for theology to solve all problems we would never pray and that he fully intended to pray before retiring that evening — theological problems notwithstanding.

Rahner writes cogently that the contemporary Christian "has a great heritage to preserve.... There is no soul without a body, there is no genuine and serious religious life without man subjecting himself to discipline and rule, exercise and duty. This institutional factor in Christian living is something which the devout Christian of the future, if he is to practice it genuinely, must decide for himself to a far greater extent than formerly.... Anyone, however, who supposes that the institutionalized practices in Christian living are already outmoded simply on the grounds that they are uncomfortable and involve strict discipline is deceiving himself and will never attain to a genuine mode of Christian living unless the grace of God rescues him ... from his impoverished and diminished form of existence, which has only a coloring of Christianity. Certainly there is no commandment of God or the Church directing us to say our prayers precisely when we get up or go to bed, or before meals. He who really is a man of prayer without these praiseworthy Christian customs may in all Christian freedom regard himself as dispensed from them. But will he be a man of prayer? Will he be able to lay the supremely decisive moments of his life before God in prayer if in his everyday life prayer is simply the outcome of a momentary prompting or merely the 'liturgical' prayer of the Church's public services, or if he has not previously fixed his own times of prayer which he voluntarily engages himself to observe? The more complex techniques of Yoga are considered reasonable, yet the old Christian methods of prayer and meditation, as for example the rosary, are regarded as unmodern.... Many instances of such institutional practices of devotion, even such as were or are common to the entire Church — one is thinking of the prescriptions of fasting, abstinence, fasting before receiving communion, holy water in the home, etc. — may be susceptible of change, and may actually need it.... But must the life of the Christian of the future be on that account actually devoid of any such formation by the Christian institutions? Why should there not be continuity between past and future in that the custom of having established usages which are Christian and human could be discovered and practiced afresh?... Where the power of Christian living to embody itself in concrete practices of devotion is plainly flagging then Christian living itself is beginning to die."[35]

To a young man who dismissed praying the rosary as meaningless and as laughable as praying a cookbook recipe, Rahner writes that he suspects the man never actually prayed the rosary.[36] "If you had already tried it fairly often, then perhaps it would have occurred to you that in the very monotony of this prayer — aside from the genuine essence of prayer as such — there is contained an enormous power for stillness, composure, and courage to be by yourself, far from all your daily pursuits."[37] This same young man wrote that a "true believer doesn't need symbolic activities for his faith," a remark that Rahner branded as "frightfully silly."[38] "Aren't you a person of body and soul?" Rahner asks. "Isn't it necessary for the innermost reality at the core of your being to express itself bodily? Can you do without art and music? After all, what happens in these are always and really only symbolic activities through which a person expresses the most interior events of his or her existence. Why should it be different in our relationship to God?"[39]

Eucharistic Devotion

Rahner maintains that the Church has a history of piety. Ancient customs may change throughout this history and yet keep their ancient identity. It is important for the Church's life, therefore, to return continually to the ancient sources. One should not be indifferent to ancient devotions by simply giving them up as outdated. Often they offer the Church new possibilities and tasks for her future life.

For this reason, Rahner looks askance at the decline in such eucharistic devotions as silent adoration before the tabernacle, the Corpus Christi processions, the use of the monstrance, genuflection before the Blessed Sacrament, and a period of thanksgiving after receiving Communion. He seems to regret the fading away of the custom of blessing oneself or making the sign of the cross when one passes in front of a church, yet thinks it best not to try to revive that devotion. "However, real worship of the sacrament of the altar, both in private and in common," he writes, "even apart from Holy Communion, must not disappear.... It is part of the Catholic faith that Jesus Christ is truly present with his divinity and his humanity under the eucharistic species. It is true that this presence under symbols of human food points to the reception and enjoyment of this eucharistic nourishment.... True, compared with the real reception of the heavenly bread, such adoration is not the highest point of the sacramental happening. But it is a practice that follows legitimately from the Catholic belief in the true presence of the Lord in the sacrament."[40] For this reason, "we should see Christians kneeling in church, alone and in silence, before the tabernacle in which the bread of life is kept, so that it may be received.... The sanctuary lamp of our Catholic churches continues to invite us to a silent lingering before the mystery of our redemption."[41]

Devotion to the Virgin Mary

Rahner wrote much about genuine devotion to Our Lady because he viewed her as the perfectly redeemed one and as Christ's perfect disciple. Her significant role in salvation history as the Mother of God, too, should not be underestimated by Christians. In an essay written only a year before his death, Rahner says that "by praising and honoring Mary, the Church welcomes and calls by name that which God has done and continues to do for her until the end of time. The Church fulfills Mary's prophecy that all generations will call her blessed because God has looked graciously upon the lowliness of his handmaid. And as the Church thus praises Mary, she becomes actually, and not just theoretically, aware of her own vocation: that God may become all in all in her and that precisely in this way the blessed perfection of human beings may be achieved."[42]

Although Rahner eschews pseudo-Marian developments, he writes that "one should, however, exercise a certain tolerance in regard to harmless excesses in Marian devotion."[43] To an interviewer, Rahner said: "When we pray to Mary, we open ourselves to her solidarity with us, the solidarity that flows from her role in the history of salvation and that has been brought to its fulfillment in God.... When anyone prays a Hail Mary and does it truly from the heart, then that is certainly much more significant than all the theological language that we have used in this conversation."[44]

Devotion to the Saints

One of the marks of the true Church is holiness. As the Church of the absolute savior in which God's self-offer and acceptance become one by God's grace, she must attest to the real and final victory of God's grace which established her. When the Church declares a person a saint, she actualizes her very being by stating her holiness concretely, in actual flesh and blood. The reward of the Church's actual saints belongs to her innermost being. To Rahner, the Church must canonize saints to be Church.

The saints create new modes of Christian life and evince the history of the Church's appropriation of God's grace and holiness. "Herein lies the special task which the canonized saints have to fulfill for the Church," Rahner writes. "They are the initiators and the creative models of the holiness which happens to be right for, and is the task of, their particular age. They create a new style; they prove that a certain form of life and activity is a really genuine possibility; they show experimentally that one can be a Christian even in 'this' way."[45] They give witness to the astonishing fact that God's grace incarnates itself in human beings not only to permeate the world temporarily but also to remain in this unique way for all eternity.

The Church imposes no obligation on Christians to pray to the saints even in her official liturgical veneration of them. In line with Church teaching, however, Rahner states that it is good and beneficial to pray to the saints. Veneration of the saints has an official place in the Church, which must not be destroyed by misguided reforms. "One should not," Rahner says, "elevate one's own lack of interest in the saints or in particular saints to a principle that is binding on all Christians.... It is ultimately a sign of human development when we can admit with gratitude that another person really means something to us. The areas in which this is the case can, naturally, vary considerably. It can even include salvation and grace and our relationship to God."[46] For example, a father may worry much about providing for his family and for that reason be devoted to St. Joseph. This devotion may be secondary to his overall spiritual life, yet foster a more intense Christian life and a deeper love of Christ.

Not to pray to the saints, in fact, may be an implicit denial of eternal life or an inhumane indifference to the enormous past suffering of the dead. Praying to the saints gives witness to our universal solidarity with the human race and the one human history. Although the emotional atmosphere of our age may make us more prone to a spirituality of silent submission to the ineffable, unfathomable mystery of God, Rahner reminds us that "only persons who love others and include them lovingly in their lives can truly achieve...immediacy to God."[47] We cannot exclude other human beings from our immediacy to God.

Rahner also calls attention to a person's social nature, to human solidarity with Jesus, and Jesus' solidarity with all humanity. Human beings are thus able to communicate directly with God only in the "communion of saints" in and with Jesus. "When we speak of venerating the saints," Rahner writes, "we simply mean that love of our fellow humans is extended to all, not only those people we actually meet in our everyday lives. Truly Christian love of our fellow human beings must embrace all, including the dead."[48] Venerating the saints, therefore, expresses our freely realized solidarity with all human beings — even the dead — and is also by implication an act of worship of God. Within this context Rahner praises "the apparently bizarre habit that many pious Christians have of praying for and to the forgotten 'poor souls'"[49] and to the custom in other world religions of reverencing one's ancestors.

Anonymous Prayer

Rahner maintains that an anonymous form of Christian prayer can be found even outside of explicit Christianity. The agnostic or atheist, for example, who sacrifices self for another or who surrenders to his or her deepest mystery is praying. "When and where a person accepts himself in the totality of his existence," Rahner writes, "and so experiences himself as the one confronted with the incomprehensible mystery embracing his existence and letting him submerge himself more and more deeply in this mystery in knowledge and freedom, he is living out what prayer really is and means, and he experiences what is meant by God as the ground of all reality and all self-reflection in personhood."[50] Thus, Rahner considers prayer, faith, implicit or explicit surrender to the mystery of life, and the primordial experience of God to be inexorably linked.

Conclusion

Let us conclude this chapter with a selection from Rahner's prayer "God of My Life."[51] He prays, "Lord, how helpless I am when I try to talk to You about Yourself! How can I call You anything but the God of my life? And what have I said with that title, when no name is really adequate? I'm constantly tempted to creep away from You in utter discouragement, back to the things that are more comprehensible, to things with which my heart feels so much more at home than it does with Your mysteriousness.

"And yet, where shall I go? If the narrow hut of this earthly life with its dear, familiar trivialities, its joys and sorrows both great and small — if this were my real home, wouldn't it still be surrounded by Your distant Endlessness? Could the earth be my home without Your far-away heaven above it?

"Suppose I tried to be satisfied with what so many today profess to be the purpose of their lives. Suppose I defiantly determined to admit my finiteness, and glory in it alone. I could only begin to recognize this finiteness and accept it as my sole destiny, because I had previously so often stared out into the vast reaches of limitless space, to those hazy horizons where Your Endless Life is just beginning.

"Without You, I should founder helplessly in my own dull and groping narrowness. I could never feel the pain of longing, not even deliberately resign myself to being content with this world, had not my mind again and again soared out over its own limitations into the hushed reaches which are filled by You alone, the Silent Infinite. Where should I flee before You, when all my yearning for the unbounded, even my bold trust in my littleness, is really a confession of you?...

"But when I love You, when I manage to break out of the narrow circle of self and leave behind the restless agony of unanswered questions, when my blinded eyes no longer look merely from afar and from the outside upon Your unapproachable brightness, and much more when You Yourself, O Incomprehensible One, have become through love the inmost center of my life then I can bury myself entirely in You, O mysterious God, and with myself all my questions....

"God of my life, Incomprehensible One, be my life. God of my faith, who leads me into Your darkness — God of my love, who turns Your darkness into the sweet light of my life, be now the God of my hope, so that You will one day be the God of my life, the life of eternal love."

Notes

1. "Warum uns das Beten nottut," *Leuchtturm* 18 (1924–25): 10–11, and reprinted in *Sehnsucht nach dem geheimnisvollen Gott*, ed. Herbert Vorgrimler (Freiburg im Breisgau: Herder, 1990), 78–80. Because this text has never appeared in English, I am most grateful to Bruce Gillette for his excellent translation.

WHY WE NEED TO PRAY

How is your heart supposed to be?

Just as the holy, eternal one wanted, as he gave you to be, as he draws and guides and warns you in his holy grace....

Just as the heart of Christ, full of love and the holy power to sacrifice....

Just as you yourself desired when God's spirit filled you, your vision was clearer for your life and its task, and you demanded love which is capable of everything, understands everything....

For the strength to become everything for others, for the strength to lose yourself to serve others....

This is how you are supposed to be. Try to remember what it is about the eternal will of the incomprehensible God that you are holy, what it is about the example of him who died that you may be holy, about your heart's desire to become holy...and then say:

Is your heart like this? Is God's will in you action and truth? Is your interior man renewed in Christ Jesus? Is the urging of your heart life?...How will you be capable of this, completely capable? Always loyal without halfheartedness and cowardliness?

You must pray! We must pray! If we don't pray, we'll remain stuck to the things of the earth, we'll become petty as they, narrow as they, become crushed by them, sold to them, because we gift our love, our heart to them. We must pray! Then we are far from the petty everyday which makes us petty and narrow. Then we come near to God and become capable "ad attingendum Creatorem ac Dominum nostrum, of reaching our Creator and Lord."

Whoever comes near to God, God comes near to him (James 4:8). When he, however, communicates himself to his creature and encompasses it for his love and for his praise, then he lets the soul realize how vain, empty, and weak it is, filled by the vanities of its narrow existence, full of fear of the pain and suffering of the cross, full of small-minded pride and narrow selfishness....

Then at his time, when it pleases him, HE makes the soul light, illuminated, so that it understands what God wants and his ways, so that it desires a heart which is believing, full of strong hope, full of love which never ceases, desires a heart which is wide and selfless and pure.

Then the Lord fills his soul with grace-power so that it may fulfill in works what it desired and praised in prayer. That it will become strong to do everything and suffer everything. Then HE will give it the Spirit of God who will "come to the aid of its weakness." Who loves it so that it forgets to lust after the love of the world. Who consoles it with his joy. Who is its "pledge of eternal life."

That's how the heart that prays will become. For whoever comes near to God, he becomes one spirit with HIM. But God's Spirit is: "LOVE, JOY, PATIENCE, KINDNESS, FAITHFULNESS, GENTLENESS, SELF-CONTROL" (Gal. 5:22). This is what our heart becomes when we pray in the Spirit of God.

2. Albert Raffelt, ed. (New York: Crossroad Publishing Co., 1984).
3. *Prayers for a Lifetime,* 163–65.

Prayer for the Reunion of All Christians

God, cause and moving force of all unity, we cry out to You and ask You to grant the Christian churches which are separated from each other that unity which conforms to the will of our Lord, Jesus Christ. We know, of course, that we ourselves have to do all that is possible for us to make this unity a reality, for the split between the Christian churches came about through us, not through You. But precisely this task of ours is nevertheless the gift of Your grace which alone can grant the desire for and the achievement of that unity. And therefore all our efforts can begin again and again only with the prayer: grant what You ask of us.

When all Christian churches profess a triune God, one Lord and Redeemer Jesus Christ, when we are all baptized into You, the triune God, and are born again to eternal life in the power of Your divine Spirit, Who (so we hope) has already taken possession of us in the depth of our being, then there already does exist among us Christians that divine unity which You Yourself are; and when we pray for the unity which is yet to come, then we mean a unity of churches as an embodied historical fact, which has its source in that ultimate unity which is already given as testimony to the world and in history that the One Church can truly and clearly be the sacrament of redemption of the world. The unity of the churches is our task. . . .

Grant us the foresight and the wisdom in our powerless activity so that we do not cause yet more division within the churches through our arrogant zeal for unity. Make the leaders of the churches clear-sighted and courageous so that they feel more of a responsibility to the unity of the churches in the future than to the independence of their churches in the past. Make them daring because in the history of the Church something that is really new and great arises only when it is not completely legitimized by the past alone. Give them the joyous conviction that much more from the past can be gathered into the One Church by all the churches than is thought possible by a vision made shortsighted and fearful by the fact that what is to be gathered in was once the cause of division. Grant those in positions of responsibility in the Church the conviction that unity does not mean uniformity, by which one Church alone becomes the complete law for all the others, but rather reconciled diversity of the churches....

Holy and Merciful God, grant us the full intention for unity which You demand of us. And, if our heart accuses us of possessing too little of the powerful Spirit of Unity, then we may nevertheless hope that this sinful weakness of ours remains enveloped by Your mercy and in that unity of Christians which You already bestowed on us. Amen.

4. Trans. James M. Demske, S.J. (Westminster, Md.: Newman Press, 1960). The prayers in this out-of-print book can now be found in *Prayers for a Lifetime,* ed. Albert Raffelt (New York: Crossroad Publishing Co., 1984).

5. Trans. Bruce Gillette (Collegeville, Minn.: Liturgical Press, 1997).

6. Robert Kress, *A Rahner Handbook* (Atlanta: John Knox Press, 1982), 94.

7. See *Karl Rahner — I Remember,* esp. 64 and 103. Also see *Karl Rahner in Dialogue,* 242.

8. Ibid., 212.

9. *Faith in a Wintry Season,* 120.

10. *Christian at the Crossroads,* 53.

11. This is a constant theme throughout Rahner's writings. For example, see "Man in the Presence of Absolute Mystery," *Foundations of Christian Faith,* 44–89.

12. For the source of the remarks which follow, see "Prayer," *Encyclopedia of Theology,* 1268–77.

13. *Faith in a Wintry Season,* 132.

14. "The Possibility and Necessity of Prayer," *Christian at the Crossroads,* 54.

15. Ibid., 55.

16. "Is Prayer Dialogue with God?" *Christian at the Crossroads,* 66–67.

17. "On the Theology of the Incarnation," *TI IV,* 113.

18. "The Apostolate of Prayer," *TI III,* 210.

19. "Christian Living Formerly and Today," *TI VII,* 16.

20. "The Possibility and Necessity of Prayer," *Christian at the Crossroads,* 58–59.

21. "Prayer in the Everyday," *The Need and the Blessing of Prayer,* 46–47. Translation emended.

22. *The Need and the Blessing of Prayer,* 38.

23. *Mein Problem: Karl Rahner antwortet jungen Menschen* (Freiburg im

Breisgau: Herder, 1982), 38–41. For an alternate English translation, see *Is Christian Life Possible Today?* 36–39.

24. *The Need and the Blessing of Prayer,* 2–3 and 7–9.

25. The sources for the remarks which follow can be found in "Prayer Too Is Action," *Opportunities for Faith: Elements of a Modern Spirituality,* trans. Edward Quinn (New York: Seabury Press, 1974), 74–75. This volume will henceforth be referred to as *Opportunities for Faith.* Also see "Zur Theologie des beschaulichen Ordensleben," *Jetzt — Ordensfrauen — Ordensleben — Kirche/Information — Konfrontation* (Vienna) 2 (1983): 5–6.

26. "Prayer Too Is Action," *Opportunities for Faith,* 75. Translation emended.

27. Ibid., 75. Translation emended.

28. Ibid., 74. Translation emended.

29. Ibid., 75. Translation emended.

30. Ibid.

31. See *Bekenntnisse,* 52–53.

32. "On the Evangelical Counsels," *TI VIII,* trans. David Bourke (New York: Herder and Herder, 1971), 167.

33. *Faith in a Wintry Season,* 19.

34. Ibid., 163.

35. "Christian Living Formerly and Today," *TI VII,* 9–10. My emphasis.

36. *Is Christian Life Possible Today?* 45.

37. Ibid., 47. Translation emended.

38. Ibid., 49.

39. Ibid. Translation emended.

40. "Eucharistic Worship," *TI XXIII,* trans. Hugh M. Riley and Joseph Donceel, S.J. (New York: Crossroad Publishing Co., 1992), 115.

41. Ibid., 115–16.

42. "Courage for Devotion to Mary," *TI XXIII,* 139.

43. *Faith in a Wintry Season,* 87.

44. Ibid., 91.

45. "The Church of the Saints," *TI III,* 100.

46. *Faith in a Wintry Season,* 88–89.

47. *The Courage to Pray,* 57.

48. Ibid., 61–62.

49. Ibid., 86.

50. "The Possibility and Necessity of Prayer," *Christian at the Crossroads,* 52.

51. *Prayers for a Lifetime,* 8–14.

Chapter 5

Karl Rahner — Preacher of the Good News

Rahner maintains that he did not enter the Society of Jesus to become a scholar or a professor. He wished only to "minister to people" and viewed "the mission of the Society of Jesus . . . [as] the preaching of the Gospel at home and in actual missionary lands."[1] Rahner preached almost daily for much of his fifty-two years of priestly life. The priest, to him, is not primarily a theologian but one ordained by the Church to preach and to celebrate God's efficacious word. Only because there is preaching does theology exist, not vice versa. In fact, theology would cease if it severed its link to the preaching and proclamation of God's word of love.

Preaching the Good News

Rahner takes seriously Jesus' claim that his message is indeed "good news," or "gospel," essentially addressed to the poor person (Matt. 11:5). In this context, the poor person is essentially one who comprehends oneself as a sinner, as one deserving to be rejected by God. To such a person Jesus says that the gracious reign of God is now present because Jesus himself is here, that this world thought to be already repudiated by God has in fact been efficaciously liberated by him.

Of course, the New Testament extended the meaning of gospel to the communication of good news which occurred in Jesus Christ and is attested to by his disciples. Its content as the joyful message from God to human beings preached by the Church came to include Jesus' person, life, death, and resurrection.

When asked by an interviewer why this news is "good," Rahner replied: "I think that in all human experiences of individual realities, their finitude is ultimately experienced along with them.... All human things...ultimately display...an inability to fulfill the total 'capacity' of the human being.... If Christianity ultimately (I say 'ultimately,' not 'alone') announces that the absolute, infinite, holy, and living God is the total fulfillment of human existence, then with that comes a joy and a fulfillment of a fundamental kind that essentially...is in itself unsurpassable.... Christianity preaches an absolute joy — one can also say, an absolute future, an unlimited reality. This, then, is in an absolute sense 'good news.'"[2]

Preaching, to Rahner, is the proclamation of God's word by those commissioned by the Church in Christ's name. More than mere instruction into hidden truths or simply the teaching of abstract morality, true preaching efficaciously proclaims God's eternal plan for human salvation in Jesus Christ. Through the Church's preaching God offers both the proclamation of the truth and the gift of hearing it as truth. The word is no mere human word but the very word of God and Christ. By being spoken and heard, this word efficaciously brings about what it signifies: the offer of the grace of faith.

Preaching is also intrinsically connected to God's word which the Church addresses through the sacraments to the individual in his or her particular religious situation. The summit of preaching is the proclamation of God's consummate saving act of Christ's cross and resurrection made efficaciously present in the Eucharist. Rahner emphasizes the inextricable link between the service of God's word and the celebration of the Eucharist.

The Church preaches not a word which may be surpassed by some future prophet, but God's irrevocable and unsurpassable word promised by God himself in his own Son as his victorious self-utterance. Thus the word is an event which embodies what it says. "By the word of the gospel," Rahner writes, "a true presence of Christ is already...achieved wherever the word of the gospel is preached in power and heard in a spirit of faith.... Christ (as he who was crucified and rose again on our behalf) imparts himself to us...in an act of divine self-bestowal, and thereby makes himself present in preacher and hearer alike."[3]

Thus, to Rahner, the presence of Christ takes place in the Christian community through the word that is heard and believed — and, of course, in the effective reception of Christ's Body and Blood and in the practical love of the members of the community for one another. However, the Gospel is not merely preached in the community as gathered but is itself the basis for this state of being gathered together. To Rahner, the community takes place because of the Eucharist, Christian love, and the preached word. Preaching creates community.

Preaching and the Priesthood

For these reasons, Rahner insists that "there must be good preaching. To have good preaching, one must first have studied good theology. And there must be vital, devout, and radical Christians who then preach."[4]

Given this emphasis and context, one may understand why Rahner links the priesthood so closely to preaching and to the sacraments as the condensed word of God. What he says requires no commentary: "A priest is one sent by Christ, an apostle of the eternal God with one message that far surpasses any and all earthly duties and possibilities. This message is: There is a God and this incomprehensible One wants to be a part of our lives. Even if he caused an entire galaxy light years away to explode, he is still with me, loves me, embraces me, will make my existence eternal, and will grace me definitively with himself and his own eternal life. The word in which God commits himself to us must be spread. It must attest that through Jesus, the crucified and risen one, it has an irrevocable, eternal validity. Men must be commissioned for that task....

"God's grace and his irrevocable self-communication to us has appeared bodily, definitively, and irrevocably to us in Jesus of Nazareth, the crucified and risen one. This good news must be proclaimed. This word is of course a word in which the proclaimed reality itself as summoning, saving, and freeing should reach people. It is therefore a word which of itself brings with it the proclaimed reality. And for that reason is this word ultimately also...a 'sacramental word.' And if for this reason a priest is also one who dispenses the sacraments, the one who presides at Jesus' Last Supper in which the crucified one in his power is present, then he is not a magician of various out-dated rituals, but precisely the one who proclaims to people the ultimately incomprehensible, eternal, yet sanctifying God. If a priest cannot understand this, then he has no understanding of his priestly vocation. Then perhaps he should have become a social worker instead.

"Of course I admit that it is not easy for today's priest to deliver and to formulate the message of the Gospel and of the Church in such a way that he himself grasps what an enormously blessed message he thereby really proclaims. I admit too that it is not easy to preach this message in such a way that contemporary people understand it. Of course if the priest knows only how to repeat boring catechism-like homilies, or only has recourse to sociopolitical criticism of contemporary conditions, then of course he finds it difficult to comprehend that he is, so to speak, a 'guru' of the love of God — not by his own presumptuous authority but truly by God's interior blessing and empowerment.

"By all means there are many people...who feel the need to aim for more out of life than just making money or being able to travel. After all there are people who yearn for God's incomprehensibility and eternity. And to these the priest says: the incomprehensible optimism which you by no means attempt to be capable of out of your own power is your possibility, yes even your holy duty. You are a person of eternity, of absolute longing, of unlimited hope. You can and should be that because we have experienced the everlasting and irrevocable love of God in Jesus Christ which has blown away all your limitations."[5]

Preaching and Theology

It should be clear, therefore, why Rahner insists upon good preaching. In fact, it is instructive that this profound theologian subordinates theology to preaching. Theology must serve the Church's main mission: preaching. "All theologies and Churches must learn," he says, "...to bear witness to the Gospel of Jesus Christ in a way that is credible and intelligible. ...When viewed as a whole, [theology] has no other task than to investigate the question of how the Gospel can be *preached* in a way that awakens and claims the allegiance of faith."[6]

On the other hand, Rahner never advocated the popular 1930s theological thesis which originated at the University of Innsbruck. It declared that in addition to a scientific theology based on philosophical-theological reflection there should also be an essentially different "kerygmatic theology" which aims directly at preparing priests for pastoral ministry, especially for preaching. On this matter he even disagreed with his brother Hugo who had published the influential *A Theology of Proclamation*.[7]

Rahner maintains that *all* theology must serve the Church's kerygma, that is, the fruitful and efficacious preaching of God's saving message by the Church. A purely theoretical, unengaged theology cannot and should not exist. However, Rahner concedes that the advocates of kerygmatic theology had put their finger on a fundamental weakness in the existing scientific theology: it does not clearly serve the purposes of a vital preaching that reaches the contemporary person in his or her religious needs.

Nonetheless Rahner insists that "the present system of theological teaching at universities and seminaries...cannot withdraw from interdisciplinary dialogue and conflict and the consequent requirement of responsible scholarship and science."[8] He emphasizes, therefore, "the need for every future priest and preacher of the Word of God to reflect as intensively as possible upon the content of faith being preached."[9] In short, Rahner never accepted the Innsbruck thesis because of his view that "the strictest theology, the most passionately devoted to reality alone and ever on the alert for new questions, the most scientific theology, is itself in the long run the most kerygmatic."[10] He once told me that he feared the "Americanization" of theology, that it be packaged for and valued only if it produced quick results.

Painfully aware of the contemporary problems in theological training, Rahner asks: "Isn't it possible to imagine, given all the freedom and possibilities for forming young theologians, that the first year or two would be spent not in scholarly, narrowly academic study, but under the guidance of a 'master'? This master could be a combination of theologian and spiritual guru who could communicate to the young theologian what exactly Christianity, spiritual life, prayer, receiving the Eucharist, and basic theological reflection (reflection on the possibility of Christianity which is intellectually honest and sober) are all about."[11] Again we see his concern that educated Christians savor their faith and be able to justify it intellectually.

Theologians must remember that they reflect upon the *Church's* faith and that their thinking must have an inner continuity with the Church's faith consciousness. This requires them to be traditional in the best sense of that term. Attentive to the Church's genuine teaching authority, they think as members of the Church who respect their ecclesial discipline. The theologian is no Lone Ranger.

Rahner would not deny, however, that theology must have a respectful critical function with respect to both the Church's overall faith consciousness and to the Church's official teaching authority. However, Rahner views this critical function as "an inner function of faith of the Church's faith and of the Church's own *self*-actualization and so right from the start stands in an inner relationship to the Church's faith consciousness and at the same time also to the officially taught and officially objectified Church's faith consciousness."[12] These words come from a theologian who is no papal lackey, eschews a Roman mentality in the narrow sense, and considers dissent an important element in the Church's life. But they also come from someone who was no friend of theologians who attempt to distance themselves from the official Church.

A cartoon sent to Rahner amused him. "As you see," he says, "at the top of the cartoon is a theological atomic physicist who's supposed to be me. What it means is that I speak about things that no one understands. Beneath me sit the so-called multipliers. They are the ones who are expected to hand on what I say. Beneath them sit the popularizers who spend their time putting what the multipliers say into simple language. Below them, in the pulpit, is an individual popularizer who preaches to the Christian people what needs to be said there. Nearby sits Jesus, who listens to what is being translated from what I've concocted, and he says: 'I don't understand.' That's just the way it is when you teach theology."[13]

Thus Rahner never apologizes for his often highly abstract, speculative theology. He defends deep theological thinking. He points to the abstruse, difficult language in the physical sciences and asks why there should not be an equivalent in theology. "For example," he explains, "if you study physics, you will soon formulate and understand sentences that I certainly will not understand. Therefore I believe that if there is a theological science which has to reflect upon, make more precise, and express this or that matter, in which the average churchgoer usually is uninterested, nor understands, then it is not something to get upset about."[14]

When an interviewer mentioned the old joke that some day his brother Hugo would translate his works into German, Rahner had the last laugh. He pointed out Hugo's strong points as a good scholar of patristics and of Ignatian spirituality, but his weakness in speculative theology. Rahner said simply that his brother was incapable of the task.[15] Moreover, that Rahner received the 1973 Sigmund Freud prize for scholarly prose from the German Academy for Language and Literature attests to his often beautiful use of the German language.

When praised by an interviewer who called attention to Rahner's four thousand publications, he replied: "Even earlier I always stressed that in point of fact by profession I never claimed to be a scientific researcher either in philosophy or in theology. I never practiced theology as a sort of art for art's sake. I think I can say that my publications usually grew out of pastoral concern. But in comparison to professional scholars I have remained a theological dilettante."[16] "I am no 'scholar,'" he protested. "In this work of theology, I only want to be a man, a Christian, and, as much as possible, a priest of the Church. Perhaps a theologian cannot desire anything else. In any case the science of theology, as such, was never important to me."[17] Asked a few years before his death which encomium most pleased him, he replied: "I am a priest and a theologian, and that's it, isn't it?" He also underscored that "the pastoral concern of proclaiming the Christian faith for today has been the normative aspect of my work."[18]

One commentator writes: "Rahner is a great *pastoral* theologian *precisely because* he is one of the greatest *systematic* theologians of this century.... According to Rahner, like Bonaventure and the great medievals, pastoral and spiritual theology are not something added on to a systematic theology with which they have little or no connection. Spiritual and pastoral theology are moments of the same unified theological activity from which systematic theology arises."[19] I would prefer to say that Rahner is the theological giant of our age because his theology always remains rooted in his Jesuit, priestly, and pastoral experience. In large part his theology reflects upon his own lived Ignatian spirituality, the lived faith of the world Church, and the living questions rooted in the hearts of those he encountered. His theology is in part an attempt to proclaim Christianity's good news to the contemporary person in a way that touches this person's heart.

Rahner considers his homilies and pious works as important as his better known *Theological Investigations*. In fact, he preached as often as he could during the time he wrote the them. In addition, his hand can be found in the impressive *Handbuch der Verkündigung* ("Handbook of Preaching"). I would thus suggest that Rahner the priest, the pastor, and the preacher is present even in his most difficult works.

Contemporary Preaching

Contemporary preaching must take seriously that we live in an age of the death of God, an age from which God is seemingly absent. "Wintry faith," "troubled faith," the Christian "night of faith" — which make Rahner sympathetic to contemporary atheism and agnosticism — are frequent themes in his writings. The preacher should be attentive to the catechism of the human heart, to the troubled faith which plagues so many Christians. "Wouldn't it help many in their individual history of faith," he writes, "and better enable them to stand firm in their faith if right off something were said by way of introduction to those listening to the sermon on faith about the free, personal, subjective side of faith and its history: faith as enduring God's silence; the 'night' of faith; the seeming 'shrinking' of faith as a real compression of faith; faith (despite everything that can be said about Christianity's content) as silence concerning God; recognizing the Lord only in the 'breaking of the bread' for the 'stranger' (Luke 24:31); the continuing resurrection of faith from the grave of unbelief, and the like."[20]

Rahner believes that our contemporary heterogeneous and pluralistic culture has become more interested in making the world more humane and less interested in an afterlife. The Christian cultural supports of yesteryear hardly exist. Experiences of God seem less in evidence. Rahner suggests that Christianity shift its preaching somewhat from the "vertical" to the "horizontal," that is, from the heavenly to the earthly — without betraying its own basic truths and falling into an un-Christian pseudo-horizontalism.

To Rahner, only love is believable. The person who loves his or her neighbor truly experiences God. Thus, "nowadays in its preaching to man," Rahner writes, "the Church should cry out to him 'Love thy neighbor! Love him with a love that transcends the immediate circumstances of your own private life which are constantly suspected of being tainted by egotism! Love him even when this love, in its ultimate consequences, appears to you to amount to a fatal surrender of yourself! Only then will you keep peace with the times in learning deeply what is meant by God and love for God! For this you have to surrender yourself in an act of unreserved trust to this single moment of your existence.' And if the Church were to cry this message out to modern man, then she would simply be preaching that ultimate and essential truth which she has all along been attempting to bring home to man."[21]

Love of neighbor will sometimes demand a Christian sociopolitical and sociocritical involvement to change unjust social structures which oppress people. Strong involvement in social and political affairs should be an integral part of the faith of many Christians. Yet Rahner cautions: "After all, God does exist, and we do have a personal relationship with him, and there is God's personal judgment after each one's death. One cannot dismiss all these things in favor of a sociopolitical and sociocritical involvement.... Don't embrace socialism, properly understood, but consider that what is 'genuinely Christian' implies a personal relationship with the living God, who is not merely an old fashioned cipher for 'humanity.' "[22]

In fact Rahner has rather harsh words for those who would reduce Christianity to something only for this world. He also criticizes those who would *use* God to further human goals. The "most dangerous heresy," he maintains, is "to believe in God only when he helps us, or rather when he should help us.... [You] must adore God for his own sake, unless you want to fall into the emptiness of disillusionment and ultimate nothingness."[23] We exist for God — not vice versa.

The preacher, to Rahner, should also be aware that preaching proceeds from faith and that he himself must hear the word of God in a spirit of faith. The good preacher should realize that he often preaches to people who are Christian only in name, have not really heard God's word with their hearts, and are more in tune with secular culture than with Christianity. Contemporary preaching therefore requires missionary, mystagogic, and ecumenical sensibilities.

Rahner suggests listening to oneself preaching and asking if what one is saying would sound Christian to a person of another Church. He cautions against novelty for novelty's sake, trying to be popular and making a name for oneself. "Every age," he writes, "has its danger which consists in the inclination to reduce Christianity to something that may appear precisely at the moment to be absolutely urgent and necessary, but something which, to a certain extent, is also conditioned by what is fashionable."[24] Rahner also warns that if the preached word never encounters contradiction, it is not God's word.

Preaching and the Inner Word

Given the views of contemporary depth psychology, "it is almost banal to have to say," Rahner writes, "that in the depths of our being we are other than we interpret ourselves to be."[25] That God's victorious grace in the crucified and risen Christ anoints the very depths of every person who has ever lived or will live is a constant Rahnerian theme. One can say that God has always preached interiorly his word of victorious and irrevocable love to the human heart. "Thus the revealed word," he writes, "does not extend our knowledge of any objects no matter how knowable and in some respects worth knowing, but aids us towards a kind of 'self-understanding,' that is, toward a knowledge concerning the depths of our actual existence created by grace.... Now this depth of man's being of which he becomes conscious in faith — still prescinding from the question as to whether he is fulfilling it or not — is established by Christ alone even before a single word of our preaching reaches man."[26] This means that God's *inner* word in Christ lives in every person prior to the preached word and is the condition of possibility of truly hearing the preached word as God's word. The Christian message of faith, Christian preaching, "is accordingly really an awakening, even though an absolutely necessary one, of that Christian self-consciousness which has already been in principle established in us with the 'anointing' which is in us."[27] In other words, the explicit word of Christian preaching evokes, deepens, and makes more explicit the implicit word God has long preached into the heart of every human being.

Within this context, the preacher must not merely presuppose the traditional formulas of the faith, but rather preach the ancient truths in a new, living way that enables their personal assimilation. He must say the old in a new way, a way in which the outer word of preaching awakens the inner word which God has poured into our hearts.

Preaching from the Pulpit

The Society of Jesus enjoys the reputation of having produced great speculative theologians and gifted preachers. And following in the footsteps of St. Ignatius of Loyola, Jesuits for the most part have distinguished between the pulpit and the seat of learning by following Ignatius's injunction to preach "safe doctrine." Rahner respects this tradition.

The good preacher, to Rahner, preaches the Church's living faith, a faith that is protected by official doctrinal and pastoral authorities. Rahner looks askance at both theologians and preachers who think it their duty to throw "bombs" at ordinary Christians and the bishops by expounding the most shocking theological positions possible and then saying, "Here, you old-fashioned dummies, see how you can handle this."[28] The preacher, to Rahner, must respect the "pious ears" of the faithful, exhibit humility vis-à-vis the Church's faith consciousness — even one somewhat limited and a bit primitive — and have a genuine love for the people of God with whom the preacher desires to share the one faith.

Despite his own love of speculative theology, Rahner insists that the pulpit is not the place for the airing of abstruse questions of controversial theology. He does this not to protect

Christians, especially educated ones, from serious theological issues or to feel superior in his professional chair to the "simple faith" put forth in the pulpit. "The real reason," he writes, "why such problems should not be canvassed in the pulpit is that here it is the word of God as guiding and vivifying that must be preached, the word that is intended to touch our consciences and hearts and changes our lives. For in the pulpit it is God's truth, albeit expressed in human words, that must be imparted, and not human problems concerning this word of God."[29]

Of course, the distinction between a pulpit and a seat of learning is difficult to maintain in certain, concrete cases. Yet the good preacher takes seriously that he preaches not himself but God's liberating word. If, in a spirit of self-effacement and submission to God's truth, he stays focused on the essence of the Christian faith as taught by the Church, he need not worry that he will be reduced to old-fashioned and cliché-ridden utterances. Moreover, "when we fail to observe the difference between the pulpit and the chair of learning," Rahner writes, "the pulpit becomes the place where heresies arise in the minds of the hearers, often against the will of the preacher."[30]

Preaching the Human Mystery

We have already seen that Rahner understands the human person as a self-conscious indefinability and mystery. The preacher must awaken Christians to their own mystery as human beings.

Rahner views the recent decades of European cultural history as a great and honorable struggle for a variety of freedoms. The dark side to this struggle, however, confuses freedom and self-destructive licentiousness. The more people reject external authority of any kind, the more they fall prey to a slavery from within. Inner impotence, loss of meaning, and radical disappointment fill their lives. Because of their quest for self-actualization, people view themselves with an almost narcissistic seriousness. On the other hand, existential philosophy and depth psychology disclose that in essence we are nothing more than the intersection of dark impersonal forces. The inner journey seems to reveal the self as only a phantasmagoria.

To Rahner, however, all this produces something definitely positive: it reveals the unfathomable depths of human interiority and discloses that rational consciousness is only the tip of an iceberg which "has hidden depths to which, although they may be part of us, we have no easy access, depths in which demons may well lurk. It is full of mysterious psychic realities behind each of which stands something even more concealed and incomprehensible. . . . Those who have attempted to ground themselves in themselves have fallen into an unfathomable abyss. And so, we have become indefinable and enigmatic to ourselves. There is within us a confusion of drives and possibilities, and we do not know which is the decisive one. How are we to understand ourselves?"[31] To Rahner, the human person is essentially mystery open to God's mystery. The preacher must communicate to Christians that they really comprehend themselves only when they surrender to God's mystery.

Christianity must of course preach more concretely the answer to this question: "How are we to understand ourselves?" It must preach both a Christian pessimism and a Christian optimism because it understands the human person as a redeemed sinner. Adam's sin *and* God's victorious offer of himself to us in Christ as irrevocable love both permeate our being. These two "existentials" (characteristics of human existence which make it specifically human) ground what Rahner calls a Christian pessimism and optimism.

Preaching Christian Pessimism

The preacher must preach a Christian pessimism because of its understanding of original sin. All human beings are born in a state of inward alienation from God which makes radical guilt a possibility. However, original sin, to Rahner, is sin only in an analogous sense. Sin, strictly speaking, can result only from the misuse of one's personal freedom. Original sin is not personal sin. Nonetheless, because the human person is spirit-in-world, a world of the one history of the human race, every person finds his or her freedom — even prior to a free decision — as situated internally and externally by the guilt of others.

Christianity teaches that "this codetermination of the situation of every person by the guilt of others is something universal, permanent, and therefore also original. There are no islands for the individual person whose nature does not already bear the stamp of the guilt of others, directly or indirectly, from close or from afar. And although this is an asymptotic ideal, there is for the human race in its concrete history no real possibility of ever overcoming once and for all this determination of the situation of freedom by guilt. Throughout its history the human race can indeed, and always will, strive anew to alter this situation of guilt, and even do this with very real successes and as an obligation, so that to neglect this obligation would itself be radical guilt before God. But according to the teaching of Christianity this striving will always remain codetermined by guilt, and even a person's most ideal, most moral act of freedom enters tragically into the concrete in an appearance which, because codetermined by guilt, is also the appearance of its opposite."[32]

The preaching of Christian pessimism must alert Christians to an undeniable fact: they have been born into a world partially made by the free sinful decisions of those preceding them. They must thus understand more clearly that they have to decide about themselves and God in a world which is codetermined by guilt and the guilty refusal of others — a world that is permanently steeped in guilt.

On the one hand, Christians have the obligation to change this situation as much as possible — their pessimism cannot be an excuse for doing nothing. On the other hand, they must also reject all idealistic, communistic false optimism about the future. Rahner believes that Christianity's "historical pessimism is also the best service toward improving the world here and now, because the utopian ideal that a world functioning in perfect harmony can be created by human beings themselves only leads inevitably to still greater violence and greater cruelty than those which persons want to eradicate from the world."[33] Christians must also develop in dialogue with Marxists a "realistic humanism"[34] which focuses on responsibility, tolerance, and the general human and moral presuppositions which must exist if humanity is to have any hope of dealing with the worldwide threats it faces. Still, to Rahner, intra-worldly utopias are impossible.

St. Paul preached a Christian pessimism (and optimism) when he said: "we are ... perplexed, but not driven to despair" (2 Cor. 4:8). Rahner sees in these words not only Paul's situation as an apostle but also "a feature of Christian life always and everywhere."[35] In fact, Rahner views radical perplexity as humanity's fundamental situation and a permanent feature of human history. History cannot follow its course without friction and blind alleys. In fact, it is nothing less than a history replete with suffering, injustice, sin, evil, and death.

Because this is humanity's fundamental situation, Christians are those who live in radical perplexity. "The Christian interpretation of human existence," Rahner writes, "says that within history it is never possible wholly and definitively to overcome the riddles of human existence and history, which we experience so clearly and painfully. Such a hope is excluded by the Christian conviction that we arrive at God's definitive realm only by passing through death, which itself is the ultimate and all-embracing enigma of human existence."[36] Thus the riddle of sin and death undergirds Rahner's understanding of Christian pessimism.

Despite the lessons of history, people fear this pessimism, reject it, and repress it. The euphoric belief in progress — that better times are ahead — stamps our age. Rahner even criticizes the Second Vatican Council document *Gaudium et Spes* (to which he contributed), because "its undertone is too euphoric in its evaluation of humanity and the human condition.... It does not insist enough on the fact that all human endeavors with all their sagacity and good will, often end up in blind alleys.... In short, as Scripture says, the world is in a bad way and it will stay that way, even if, as we are obliged to do, we fight against evil to the death.... That the Church herself is a Church of sinners, that even her true and salutary doctrines lead to riddles, that the Church too, in the final analysis, does not know exactly, clearly, convincingly how we should go about it, is not the most clearly voiced conviction of the living Church."[37]

Perplexity and pessimism about the human situation also arise because we can never fully understand the meaning of suffering and death. In his fascinating article "Why Does God Allow Us to Suffer?"[38] Rahner writes that "the incomprehensibility of suffering is part of the incomprehensibility of God.... If there is not directly or indirectly this absolute acceptance of the incomprehensibility of suffering, all that can really happen is the affirmation of our own idea of God and not the affirmation of God himself.... The true answer must still be only the incomprehensible God in his freedom and nothing else. In other words, this answer can be heard only if we surrender ourselves in unconditionally adoring love as answer to God.... There is no blessed light to illumine the dark abyss of suffering other than God himself. And we find him only when we lovingly assent to the incomprehensibility of God himself, without which he would not be God."[39]

With that Rahner rejects all facile and even subtle answers to ultimate questions about suffering. All a Christian can say about suffering is that it should not be and that its incomprehensibility is rooted in God's loving incomprehensibility. Of course a Christian must do what he or she can to reduce the amount of suffering in the world and to make it a more humane place. Perplexed, but not driven to despair, the Christian must also lovingly worship the incomprehensible God.

"That is why," writes Rahner, "it is the first task of Christian preaching to speak up for Christian pessimism.... We used to say that the Christian message must convince people of their sinfulness, which they refuse to acknowledge. Undoubtedly this continues to be a task of Christianity and of the Church. ... Preaching Christian pessimism," he adds, "is quite legitimate, because the Christian message is convinced that a great part of human suffering is caused by sin, so that, in the final analysis, to admit sin is the same as to admit suffering."[40] It is somewhat astonishing that this Christian titan views the primary task of contemporary preaching to be that of attesting to Christian pessimism.

Preaching Christian Optimism

Because Rahner never takes his eyes off God's victorious and irrevocable victory in Christ over sin and death, he also encourages the preaching of a Christian optimism. He knows that a person's radical perplexity is in fact redeemed. This is also humanity's fundamental situation, a permanent feature of its history. "Christians, helped by God's grace," Rahner writes, "let themselves fall into the abyss of God's incomprehensibility and discover that this ultimate and permanent mystery of God's incomprehensibility is itself true fulfillment, freedom, and forgiving salvation. They experience their radical fall into the abyss of divinity as their deepest perplexity. They continue to experience this darkness, always more intensely and more bitterly, in a certain sense, until the dreadful absurdity of death. They see that this experience of darkness is confirmed by the fate of Jesus. At the same time, in a mysterious paradox, they feel that this very experience is sent to them by God and is the experience of the arrival of God near them. The perplexity and the fact that it is lifted by God's grace are not really two successive stages in human existence. God's grace does not totally remove the perplexity of existence. The lifting, the 'not [being] driven to despair' (2 Cor. 4:8), accepted and filled with grace, is the real truth of the perplexity itself.

"For if it is true that one day we shall see God as he is, immediately, face to face, and if he is seen there precisely as the ineffable, unfathomable mystery that can be accepted and endured only in love, that is, in a total yielding up of self, then fulfillment for Christians is the height of human perplexity.... We remain the 'perplexed.' And even the fact that we are more than saved and liberated 'perplexity' remains mysteriously hidden from us (often or forever, I do not know). But even then the fact remains that our perplexity is redeemed."[41]

Conclusion

Jesus' two prayers on the cross express to Rahner what he means by Christian pessimism and Christian optimism. Jesus prayed not only "my God, my God, why have you forsaken me?" but also, "Father, into your hands I commend my spirit." Although Rahner says that the first task of Christian preaching centers on attesting to Christian pessimism, much in Rahner's writings speaks up for Christian optimism. The incomprehensible God of healing, forgiving love is our past, present, and future. "I believe that God," he says, "will triumph over the stupidity of malice of humanity. God will not abandon us."[42] This, of course, must be preached again and again.

It seems apposite to conclude this chapter by giving a few longer illustrations of Rahner's own preaching. The chosen selections, two homilies entitled, "You Are Dust" and "Laughter," provide a good summary of many of the themes in this chapter, especially of Rahner's convictions on Christian pessimism and optimism.

"You Are Dust!"[43]

"Mardi Gras Tuesday is over. There is a time to laugh and a time to weep (Eccles. 3:4). Now we hear the words, 'Remember, man, that you are dust, and unto dust you shall return.' With the dust of the earth the priest traces on our foreheads the sign of the cross, the sign of the Son of man, so that what we are in reality may be made perceptible in sign: persons of death and persons of redemption.

"The prayer that accompanies the distribution of ashes comes from Genesis (3:19), where the divine judgment is pronounced over all human beings, who had become sinners in their first parents. The divine judgment falls dark and hopeless over all: 'For out of the earth you were taken; you are dust and to dust you shall return.'

"To be sure, we are spirit, too. But left to its own resources, what is spiritual existence except the knowledge of things incomprehensible, the knowledge of guilt, and the knowledge that there is no way out of all this. We have enough spirit in us to know God. But what does this mean except that we know we stand before the unfathomable One whose ways are unsearchable and whose judgments are incomprehensible? What does this mean except that we stand before the holy One as lost sinners? What does this mean except that with our minds we grasp the meaning of what we are in reality: dust and ashes?

"Scripture tells us that we are like the grass of the field, an empty puff of air. We are creatures of pain and sin and of drifting perplexity, who are constantly and continually losing our way in blind alleys. Despair is always threatening us, and all our optimism is only a means of numbing our hopeless, bleak anxiety. Dust, that is what we are.

"Dust doubtlessly has an inner relationship, if not an essential identity, with another concept of both Old and New Testaments: the concept of 'flesh.' 'Flesh' certainly designates, in both testaments, the whole human being. It designates the whole person precisely in his basic otherness to God, in his frailty, in his intellectual and moral weakness, in his separation from God, which is manifested in sin and death. The two assertions, 'we are dust' and 'we are flesh,' are, then, more or less essentially similar assertions.

"From this conclusion, however, we must now go on to understand the change that the sentence 'the human person is dust' undergoes in the Christian economy of salvation. The good news of salvation rings out: 'The Word became flesh.' St. Paul said that God sent his own Son in the likeness of human, sinful flesh (Rom. 8:3). We can add to this and say that God himself has strewn his own head with the dust of the earth.... He has become flesh, flesh that suffers even unto death, transitory, fleeting, unstable dust.

"But ever since then, as Tertullian says, this *caro* has become the *cardo salutis*. Flesh has become the hinge, the pivot of salvation.... Ever since that moment, the sentence of terrifying judgment, 'dust you are,' is changed for the person of faith and love. This is not the one who despairs at the downward movement of returning into the dust, and who 'puts on the brakes' because he wants to stop this movement short of anxiety and terror. Rather, the individual of faith and love is the one who causes the movement to swing further, right into the midst of the dust and through it.... The downward motion of the believer, the descent with Christ into the dust of the earth, has become an upward motion, an ascent above the highest heaven. Christianity does not set free from the flesh and dust, nor does it bypass flesh and dust; it goes right through flesh and dust. And that is why the expression 'dust you are' is still applicable to us; rightly understood, it is a complete expression of our life.... In these words we are told everything that we are: nothingness that is filled with eternity; death that teems with life; futility that redeems; dust that is God's life forever.

"To say this is easy. To endure it is hard. But we have to endure it. In the boredom of everyday routine, in the disappointments that we experience in everything — in ourselves, in our neighbors, in the church — in the anxiety of time, in the futility of our labor, in the brutal harshness of universal history. Again and again we shall lie in the dust of our weakness, humiliated and weeping.... We shall experience again and again that we are dust. We shall not only be told this in a ceremony, but we shall experience it in life, and throughout life.... Just as the sacrament of baptism is an image and symbol of the approaching humble reality of routine everyday life and of the splendor and glory hidden therein, so too, the sacramental ashes are an image and a symbol of the approaching humble reality of everyday life, and of the splendor and glory hidden therein."

"Laughter"[44]

"By 'laughter' we do not mean the sublime heavenly joy that is the fruit of the Holy Spirit, nor the joy that 'spiritual persons' like to talk about in soft, gentle terms (a joy that can easily produce a somewhat insipid and sour effect, like the euphoria of a harmless, balanced, but essentially stunted person). No, we mean real laughter, resounding laughter, the kind that makes a person double over and slap his thigh, the kind that brings tears to the eyes; the laughter that accompanies spicy jokes, the laughter that reflects the fact that a human being is no doubt somewhat childlike and childish. We mean the laughter that is not very pensive, the laughter that ceremonious people (passionately keen on their dignity) righteously take amiss in themselves and in others. This is the laughter we mean. Is it possible for us to reflect on this laughter? Yes, indeed, very much so. Even laughable matters are very serious. Their seriousness, however, dawns only on the one who takes them for what they are: laughable.

"In the most pessimistic book of the Bible we read: 'There is a time to weep and a time to laugh; a time to mourn and a time to dance' (Eccles. 3:4). This is what laughter tells us first of all: there is a time for everything. The human being has no fixed dwelling place on this earth, not even in the inner life of the heart and mind. Life means change. Laughter tells us that if as people of the earth we wanted to be always in the same fixed state of mind and heart, if we wanted always to brew a uniform mixture out of every virtue and disposition of the soul (a mixture that would always and everywhere be just right), laughter tells us that fundamentally this would be a denial of the fact that we are created beings. To want to escape from the atmospheric conditions of the soul — the human soul that can soar as high as the heavens in joy and be depressed down to death in grief — to want to escape by running under the never-changing sky of imperturbability and insensitivity: this would be inhuman. It would be stoical, but it would not be Christian. This is what laughter tells us first of all. A praising of God is what laughter is, because it lets a human being be human.

"Laughter that springs from a childlike and serene heart... can exist only in one who is not a 'heathen,' but who like Christ (Heb. 4:15; cf. 1 Pet. 3:8) has through love for all and each, the free, detached 'sympathy' that can accept and see everything as it is.... Because there are great and small, high and low, sublime and ridiculous, serious and comical, because God wills these to exist — that is why this should be recognized, that is why everything should not be taken as being the same, that is why the comical and the ridiculous should be laughed at. But the only one who can do this is the person who does not adapt everything to himself, the one who is free from self, and who like Christ can 'sympathize' with everything; the one who possesses that mysterious sympathy with each and every thing, and before whom each can get a chance to have its say.

"But only the person who loves has this sympathy. And so, laughter is a sign of love. Unsympathetic people (people who cannot actively 'sympathize' and who thus become passively unsympathetic as well) cannot really laugh. They cannot admit that not everything is momentous and significant. They always like to be important and they occupy themselves only with what is momentous. They are anxious about their dignity, they worry about it; they do not love, and that is why they do not even laugh. But we want to laugh and we are not ashamed to laugh. For it is a manifestation of the love of all things in God. Laughter is a praise of God, because it lets a human being be a loving person.

"But it is more, this harmless, innocent laughter of the children of God. Scripture makes this small creature into a picture and likeness of God's own sentiments. So much so that we would almost be afraid to attribute to God the harsh, bitter, scornful laughter of pride. The thrones in heaven laugh (Ps. 2:4). The Almighty laughs at the wicked man, for he sees his day already approaching (Ps. 37:13). Wisdom, speaking of the ungodly, tells us that the Lord shall laugh them to scorn (Wisd. 4:18).

"God laughs. He laughs the laughter of the carefree, the confident, the unthreatened. He laughs the laughter of divine superiority over all the horrible confusion of universal history that is full of blood and torture and insanity and baseness. He laughs sympathetically and knowingly, almost as if he was enjoying the tearful drama of this earth (he can do this, for he himself wept with the earth, and he, crushed even to death and abandoned by God, felt the shock of terror). He laughs, says Scripture, and thus it tells us that an image and a reflection of the triumphant, glorious God of history and of eternity still shines in the final laugh that somewhere springs out from a good heart, bright as silver and pure, over some stupidity of this world. Laughter is praise of God because it is a gentle echo of God's laughter, of the laughter that pronounces judgment on all history.

"But it is still more, this harmless laughter of the loving heart. In the beatitudes according to Luke (6:21), this is what we find: 'Blessed are you who weep now, you shall laugh!' Of course, this laughter is promised to those who weep, who carry the cross, those who are hated and persecuted for the sake of the Son of Man. But it is laughter that is promised to them . . . not merely a gentle blessedness; an exultation or a joy that wrings from the heart tears of a surprising happiness. All this, too. But also laughter. Not only will our tears be dried up; not only will the great joy of our poor heart, which can hardly believe in eternal joy, overflow even to intoxication; no, not only this — we shall laugh! . . . Laughter is praise of God because it foretells the eternal praise of God at the end of time, when those who must weep here on earth shall laugh.

"Fools laugh, and so do the wise; despairing non-believers laugh, and so do believers. . . . Our laughter should praise God. It should praise him because it acknowledges that we are human. It should praise him because it acknowledges that we are people who love. It should praise him because it is a reflection and image of the laughter of God himself. It should praise him because it is the promise of laughter that is promised to us as victory in the judgment. God gave us laughter; we should admit this and — laugh."

Notes

1. *Karl Rahner — I Remember,* 21.
2. *Faith in a Wintry Season,* 10.
3. "The Presence of the Lord in the Christian Community of Worship," *TI X,* trans. David Bourke (New York: Herder and Herder, 1973), 78.
4. *Faith in a Wintry Season,* 12.
5. *Karl Rahner in Dialogue,* 350–51.
6. "Some Problems in Contemporary Ecumenism," *TI XIV,* trans. David Bourke (New York: Seabury Press, 1976), 253. My emphasis.
7. Trans. Richard Dimmler et al. (New York: Herder and Herder, 1968).
8. *Dictionary of Theology,* 263.
9. *Faith in a Wintry Season,* 9.
10. "The Prospects for Dogmatic Theology," *TI I,* trans. Cornelius Ernst, O.P. (Baltimore: Helicon Press, 1961), 7.
11. *Faith in a Wintry Season,* 32.
12. "Die 'Affäre' Halbfas," *Kritisches Wort: Aktuelle Probleme in Kirche und Welt* (Freiburg im Breisgau: Herder, 1970), 157. This volume henceforth referred to as *Kritisches Wort.*
13. *Karl Rahner — I Remember,* 19. The cartoon is found on page 18.
14. *Faith in a Wintry Season,* 100.
15. See *Glaube in winterlicher Zeit: Gespräche mit Karl Rahner aus den letzten Lebensjahren,* ed. Paul Imhof und Hubert Biallowons (Düsseldorf: Patmos Verlag, 1986), 13; *Karl Rahner — I Remember,* 47.
16. *Faith in a Wintry Season,* 174.
17. "Selbstporträt," *Forscher und Gelehrte,* 21.
18. *Karl Rahner in Dialogue,* 334.
19. Gerald McCool, S.J., *A Rahner Reader* (New York: Seabury Press, 1975), xxiv–xxv. McCool's emphasis.
20. For example, see *Handbuch der Pastoraltheologie,* 2d ed. (Freiburg im Breisgau: Herder, 1972), 3:523.
21. "The Church's Commission to Bring Salvation and the Humanization of the World," *TI XIV,* 309.
22. *Faith in a Wintry Season,* 104.
23. Ibid., 161 and 108.
24. Ibid., 104.
25. Ibid., 127.
26. "Priestly Existence," *TI III,* 251–52.
27. Ibid., 252.
28. "Die 'Affäre' Halbfas," *Kritisches Wort,* 154. For the source of the remarks which follow, see 154–57.

29. "Heresies in the Church Today?" *TI XII*, trans. David Bourke (New York: Seabury Press, 1974), 138.

30. Ibid., 139.

31. "The Divided and Enigmatic Nature of Humanity," *The Content of Faith: The Best of Karl Rahner's Theological Writings*, ed. Karl Lehmann, Albert Raffelt, and Harvey D. Egan, S.J. (New York: Crossroad Publishing Co., 1992), 120. This volume will henceforth be referred to as *The Content of Faith.*

32. *Foundations of Christian Faith,* 109.

33. Ibid., 109–10.

34. *Faith in a Wintry Season,* 137–40.

35. See "Christian Pessimism," *TI XXII*, trans. Joseph Donceel, S.J. (New York: Herder and Herder, 1991), 155.

36. Ibid., 157.

37. Ibid., 158.

38. *TI XIX*, 194–208.

39. Ibid., 207–8.

40. "Christian Pessimism," *TI XXII*, 157.

41. Ibid., 161–62.

42. *Faith in a Wintry Season,* 158.

43. *The Content of Faith,* 92–96.

44. Ibid., 148–52.

Chapter 6

Karl Rahner — Lover of Jesus Christ

We have already seen that Karl Rahner grew up in a "perfectly normal Christian family" and led a Christian life from his youth. As a teenager he read *The Imitation of Christ*, attended Mass regularly, and even spent time making a thanksgiving after Mass. He entered the Jesuit Order, the Society of Jesus, and lived its deeply Christocentric spirituality. Which contemporary theologian has written so much Christology, preached so much on Jesus Christ, and written prayers to him? Which contemporary theologian has written so copiously and so movingly about devotion to the Sacred Heart of Jesus? If Rahner's *Foundations of Christian Faith* may be considered a summary of what he considers important in the "hierarchy of Christian truths," then one should note that more than one-third of this book is devoted to Christology. In short, Rahner's theology and spirituality are markedly Christocentric.

Responding to an interviewer's query Rahner once said, "The center of my theology? Good Lord, that can't be anything else but God as mystery and Jesus Christ, the crucified and risen one, as the historical event in which this God turns irreversibly toward us in self-communication.... We have to remember that humanity is unconditionally directed toward God, a God which we ourselves are not. And yet, with this God, who in every respect infinitely surpasses us, with this God himself, we do have something to do; God is indeed not only the absolutely distant one, but also the absolutely near one, absolutely near, also, in his history. It is precisely because of this that God as this center at the same time makes Jesus Christ the center."[1]

The previous chapters perhaps say relatively less about Jesus

129

Christ than one would expect from Rahner. However, this chapter will show in no uncertain terms his warm, passionate love for Jesus Christ. Jesus, to Rahner, is no abstract religious ideal but a real flesh-and-blood person. It will also illustrate his refusal to reduce Jesus Christ, the God-Man, to just another charismatic human being. Because he is God's humanity in the world, Rahner says that in Jesus we find God's history and our history united. Moreover, even those who do not know Christ or who do not explicitly accept him may still anonymously die with him into God.

An Ascending Christology

Genuine Christian love for Jesus Christ must avoid two misunderstandings. The first misconception — which Rahner calls a "Jesusism" — considers Jesus as simply one of the world's many great prophets, religious founders, and religious geniuses. The second misconception views Jesus as an idea or an ideal. In this understanding Jesus is merely the symbol of God's absolute self-bestowal on the world, or the Omega of a cosmic evolutionary process, or the world soul of the Greeks, or the cipher of ideal human love. In contrast, genuine Christianity, Rahner points out, has long worshiped the real flesh-and-blood Jesus of Nazareth as the God-Man. "Ascending Christology" and "descending Christology" are the fruits of centuries of effort to understand, love, and worship Jesus Christ while avoiding these misunderstandings.

An ascending Christology is one in which "the eye of the believer in his experience of saving history alights first on the man Jesus of Nazareth, and on him in his fully human reality, in his death, in his absolute impotence and in his abiding definitive state which his reality and his fate have been brought to by God, something which we call his resurrection, his glorification, his sitting at the right hand of the Father.... The point of departure for this Christology, therefore, is the simple experience of the man Jesus, and of the resurrection in which his fate was brought to its conclusion. It is he whom the person encounters in his existential need, in his quest for salvation. And in Jesus he experiences the fact that the mystery of the human being, which it is not for the person himself to control, and which is bound up with the absurdity of guilt and death, is, nevertheless, hidden in the love of God."[2]

One begins, therefore, with the experience of the *man* Jesus. Rahner notes that Jesus is unnoticed for most of his life, leads a short public life, is a man of scandal, and dies an agonizing death on a cross. He passes up everything that most people consider essential for full self-actualization. He does not marry, has only a few close friends, is not interested in political reform, and does not cultivate the arts or the sciences. Of course, he does allow himself a few simple pleasures and does not resent the good things in life. However, "he is silent and passes by like one for whom everything in a certain sense is already dead, or at most provisional."[3] Because he lives solely for his Father's will, he considers the seemingly necessary and beautiful things of life unessential to his mission which is to *be* and to offer salvation.

The everydayness of Jesus' life, moreover, deeply impresses Rahner. "That which is amazing and even confusing in the life of Jesus," Rahner writes, "... is that it remains completely within the framework of everyday living; we could even say that in him concrete human existence is found in its most basic and radical form. The first thing that we should learn from Jesus is to be fully human! The courage to do this ... is not at all easy. . . . But if the Word of God assumed a concrete human existence in Jesus, then this must clearly be so great, meaningful for the future, and so full of possibilities, that God did not become anything else but a man just like this when he wanted to go outside of himself."[4] In short, to Rahner, man is God "outside of himself." In Christ, God has assumed the everyday.

However, even an ascending Christology must experience that "Jesus of Nazareth is ... the definitive, unsurpassable, and victorious — in other words eschatological — utterance of God to humanity. And because of this, and to the extent that it is true, Jesus cannot be subsumed into the category of prophet and religious reformer. . . . Jesus in his human lot is *the* (not *an!*) address of God to humanity, and as such eschatologically unsurpassable."[5] Christianity, to Rahner, must never forget Jesus in his human reality; on the other hand, it can never be satisfied with only a simple human encounter with the man Jesus. He was and is to be experienced by Christians not simply as another religious genius but as God's ultimate Word to us.

A Descending Christology

That Jesus Christ is the "Word made flesh" is, to Rahner, an almost self-evident statement for Christians. It is the key statement of a descending Christology — that is, one which begins with the Eternal *Word* and ends in the God-*Man*.[6]

In line with the Greek Fathers of the Church, Rahner predicates the word "God" primarily, but not exclusively, of Jesus' Father and refers to Jesus as the eternal Word incarnate. Jesus, to Rahner, is not simply God in general, but God's enfleshed Word. Because the Word is the Father's expression in the eternal Godhead, the Father's expression and revelation of himself outside the Godhead must take place through the Word. Only the Word could and did become flesh. Therefore Rahner does not share St. Augustine's view that any of the three divine Persons could have become man.

When Christians say that God became man, they assume too quickly that they understand what man is. Rahner understands the human person as an indefinability conscious of itself. The human person as spirit-in-world is essentially unlimited openness to and infinite longing for God's incomprehensible fullness — thus, a mystery open to God's mystery. And to Rahner the incarnation is possible only because God created beings who as spirit-in-world have the ability to be infinitely open to God's self-communication. Thus God could not have become a rock, plant, or animal because these creatures are not spirit, that is, open to God's infinity.

In Rahner's view, God created human nature as the ability to be God in the world. Because God has offered self to every human being, all human beings stand in radical nearness to God. However, in Jesus Christ, says Rahner, "God takes on a human nature as his own. The indefinable [human] nature,... when assumed by God as his reality, simply arrived at the point to which it always strives by nature of its essence. It is its meaning.... The incarnation of God is therefore the unique, supreme case of the total actualization of human reality, which consists of the fact that man is insofar as he gives himself up."[7] The incarnation, to Rahner, thus reveals the deepest meaning of being human. Because God created human nature with a view to the incarnation, this nature is the ability to be God in the world. Of course, only in Jesus does human nature arrive at its full potential. Only Jesus' human reality *is* God's reality in the world.

"We could now define man," Rahner writes, "...as that which ensues when God's self-utterance, his Word, is given out lovingly into the void of god-less nothing. Indeed, the Logos made man has been called the abbreviated Word of God. This abbreviation, this code-word for God is man, that is, the Son of Man and men, who exist ultimately because the Son of Man was to exist. If God wills to become non-God, man comes to be.... And if this God remains the insoluble mystery, man is forever the articulate mystery of God."[8]

Thus, the human reality of Christ is precisely what comes about when God's Logos expresses himself outside the God-head into creation. Traditional theology speaks as if God first created a human reality and then assumed it as his own. To Rahner, however, Jesus' human reality *is* God's self-emptying, self-expressing Word in the world. From the very moment of his existence, Jesus in his human reality *is* God's kenosis — and he now exists eternally as such.

To Rahner, it takes God's Word to be fully human. Only the Word's self-emptying fully actualizes the human potential to be God's existence in the world. Thus only the God-Man reveals the ultimate depths of our human nature. And because God has accepted our humanity in Christ, even non-Christians who accept fully their human mystery accept Christ. "Anyone," Rahner writes, "who accepts his own humanity in full — and how immeasurably hard that is, how doubtful whether we really do it! — has accepted the Son of Man, because God has accepted man in him."[9]

The Death of Christ

Christians confess, of course, that Jesus Christ is like us in all things, save sin. This radically free and sinless human being, as a member of the fallen race of Adam, took death upon himself in absolute freedom. He brought his whole life to fulfillment by undergoing death which since Adam is obscure, ambiguous, and the manifestation of a fallen world. In Christ, therefore, death becomes something absolutely different. "It is precisely by its darkness," Rahner writes, "that the death of Christ becomes the expression and embodiment of his loving obedience, the free transference of his entire created existence to God. What was the manifestation of sin becomes, without its darkness being lifted, the manifestation of an assent to the will of the Father which is the negation of sin."[10]

Rahner understands Christ on the cross as experiencing the full power of evil attempting to thwart his free "Yes" to the Father. Evil is fully unmasked at this point as the will to murder even God's Word. Rahner views this as Christ's descent into hell. Expressing all the misery of the sinful, God-forsaken man, the absolutely free and sinless holy One cries out, "My God, my God, why have you forsaken me?" Nonetheless, surrendering with trust and love, he also cries out: "Father, into your hands I commend my spirit."

Rahner disagrees with the traditional theological opinion that the soul at death becomes acosmic, that is, it goes somewhere not of this world. Because the human person is always spirit-in-*world*, at death he or she becomes "pancosmic," that is, enters into an even deeper, richer relationship with the one world. Thus Rahner views the dying Christ as "inserted into this whole world in its ground as a permanent determination of a real ontological kind.... To the innermost reality of the world there belongs what we call Jesus Christ in his life and death, what was poured out over the cosmos at the moment when the vessel of his body was shattered in death, and Christ became, even in his humanity, what he had always been by his dignity, the heart of the universe, the innermost center of all created reality."[11] In a sense, therefore, the entire world becomes Christ's body. Every human person is essentially spirit in a Christified world.

Rahner holds the theological position that even if human beings had not sinned the Word still would have become flesh because God creates in order to give self to the world. "In the Catholic Church," Rahner writes, "it is permitted to see the incarnation first of all, in God's primary intention, as the summit and height of the divine plan of creation, and not primarily and in the first place as the act of a mere restoration of a divine-world order destroyed by the sins of mankind, an order which God had conceived in itself without any incarnation."[12] In other words God became flesh *primarily* to share his life with us. Because of our sin, God's self-giving must also forgive, heal, and redeem us.

The incarnation, to Rahner, reaches its climax through Christ's death in which the God-Man becomes a permanent part of this world. It is the point toward which all creation is evolving, the point at which God's self-offer and its free acceptance are made one by God.[13] Christ is the irrevocable oneness of this self-offer and its acceptance, thus the God-Man. From the very beginning of creation God gave and still gives his grace in view of the incarnation. All grace is the grace of Jesus Christ. "And the grace of God and Christ," Rahner writes, "is in everything, as the secret essence of all eligible reality: it is not so easy to grasp at anything, without having to do with God and Christ — one way or another."[14]

Rahner strongly rejects the common appeasement view of the death of Christ — that only a God-Man could pay the infinite debt incurred by sinful humanity and thus appease the wrathful God demanding bloody sacrifice. God is unchanging love. God loves even sinful humanity and offers himself even prior to Jesus' actual sacrifice on the cross but in view of it because creation is Christocentric from the very beginning. Because God loves the sinner and wishes to reconcile us to him (not vice versa), the cross, in Rahner's view, is the symbol of God's irrevocable will to communicate himself to us as unconditional love.

Thus, the cross does not change God from wrathful to loving. "This by no means denies," Rahner writes, "that the holy God rejects sin absolutely and in that sense is 'angry' with the sinner. But this rejection always coexists in God with his desire to forgive and to overcome human sin. The cross, the reality of Christ, his love, his faith, his hope, his surrender to God's incomprehensibility are, however, the result of a redeeming love of God which itself has no cause outside of itself. God so loved the world that he gave his only-begotten Son, and it was not because the Son gave himself that an angry God with great effort changed his mind about the world. One need have no reservations in using the formulation of Scotus which says that God would never have permitted sin in the world if he had not loved the world in so radical a way, that sin, without becoming meaningless, would always be overcome by the fact that God willed Jesus Christ crucified and risen.... In the practical and concrete order Christians can say that if God had not willed this Jesus of Nazareth with his absolute solidarity both with sinner and with God, he never would have permitted the horror of this sinful world."[15] The cross, therefore, is the effect, not the cause of God's redemptive, healing love. "We are saved," Rahner writes, "because this man who is one of us has been saved by God, and God has thereby made his salvific will present in the world, really and irrevocably."[16]

The Resurrection of Christ

Christians confess that God's saving power raised the crucified Jesus bodily from the dead.[17] Rahner cautions, however, against conceiving resurrection as merely a resuscitation. Lazarus, for example, was resuscitated, that is, brought back to his former life, which continued on as before until he died again. Rahner understands Jesus' resurrection as the final, conclusive, definitive form of his person and his actual history before and with God. In his whole historical reality Jesus has risen to glorified, transformed perfection and immortality. Thus the risen Christ is neither a resuscitated corpse nor a spiritual idea but the fully transformed Jesus.

Through death Jesus freely hands over his entire existence to the Father, who accepts it and makes it permanently valid. This is what Rahner understands by Jesus' resurrection. "The resurrection," Rahner writes, "means the ultimate, God-given form of ... [Jesus'] earthly life belonging to history. And this history has an ultimate meaning because in the incarnation and cross of the eternal Logos it is the history of God himself."[18] The resurrection bestows upon Jesus' entire history its definitive mode of existence. And from the resurrection, one can also narrate God's definitive history.

Christian faith remains inextricably linked to Jesus' *historical* existence.[19] "When we turn to the exalted Lord in faith, in hope and in love," Rahner says, "we find none other than the crucified Jesus, in whose *death* his whole earthly life is of course integrated.... The risen Lord is the One who was crucified.... We must not render trivial the identity between the earthly Jesus and the exalted Lord.... His eternal life is rather the ultimate form of his earthly life itself.... His life in eternity is the ultimate form of his history."[20]

Thus, Christian devotion must avoid praying to the glorious Lord in a way that dissolves his genuine earthly history. It must also *avoid* turning *backwards* in imagination to Jesus' past history to pray to him "as if" he were present as fetus, baby, child, young adult, and so on. We can and must pray to the Jesus of the entire liturgical year because all the mysteries of his life have their eternal reality and validity in the Risen Lord. The Risen Lord *is* the crucified One, the One who suffered, ate the Last Supper with his disciples, performed miracles, lived a hidden life, was a child, a baby, and a fetus.

We saw above that through death Jesus became the heart and center of the world. "Everything" Rahner writes, "has become different in the true and decisive depths of all things. His resurrection is like the first eruption of a volcano which shows that in the interior of the world God's fire is already burning, and this will bring everything to blessed ardor in his light.... Already from the heart of the world into which he descended in death, the new forces of a transfigured earth are at work. Already in the innermost center of all reality, futility, sin and death are vanquished."[21] In Christ's resurrection, therefore, God has shown that he has taken all creation to himself. There is no abyss between God and world.

The core of every person's being contains the hope that his or her history of freedom will be conclusive and definitive. The human hope for absolute and total fulfillment, therefore, already includes hope of resurrection. Moreover, the "searching Christology" we *are* and live seeks that historical person whose full humanity has succeeded. Searching Christology finds what it seeks in the Risen Christ.

Thus one believes in Jesus' resurrection in the context of one's own hope of resurrection. Nonetheless one knows that this hope is not in vain only because Jesus is risen. "We therefore can and must say," Rahner says, "[that] because Jesus is risen, I believe in and hope for my own resurrection. For that reason we are now bound to interpret Jesus' resurrection as the final and conclusive form of this person and his actual history before God and with him."[22]

However, it is not enough simply to look at our own hope of resurrection to believe in Jesus' resurrection. "The Christian experience of Jesus' resurrection," Rahner writes, "remains bound to the apostolic testimony, because without that testimony our own resurrection would no longer be mediated to ourselves through Jesus, as an actual named individual. The search for the actual event toward which our own resurrection hope is directed, as its historical verification and mediation, would run into the sand without the testimony of the apostles."[23] Thus to believe that Jesus has indeed risen from the dead one must look both to one's own hope of resurrection and to the apostolic testimony to Jesus' actual resurrection mediated to us through the Church.

Rahner asks: "Do you believe that Jesus is risen from the dead, or do you believe also *because* he has risen from the dead?"[24] Christian faith, to Rahner, is essentially an Easter faith. The disciples came to believe *because* Jesus was raised from the dead. The Gospels are written from the point of view of the resurrection. They understand everything in Jesus' life and death from the perspective of his resurrection. Thus, so should we. Just as God's mighty deeds are foundational for Jewish belief, the Buddha's enlightenment experience foundational for Buddhists, and Mohammed and the Koran foundational for Muslims, so too is the resurrection foundational for Christians.

The Spirit of Jesus Christ

The history of salvation, or God's relationship with humanity, remained open and ambiguous until God uttered his irrevocable Word in Christ.[25] Would God be remote or near, harsh judge or lover, stern Lord or Father? Would we be servants or children of God? Would history fail or succeed?

The Spirit was always present and active in the world, albeit often in a hidden way. The Spirit in the Old Testament moved intermittently and mysteriously here and there, spoke through the prophets, yet provided no abiding sign of his presence and power. Yet the Holy Spirit, to Rahner, always and everywhere guided the course of salvation history as the secret dynamism of graced creation. This Spirit directed the history of salvation to the high point of God's intimacy with his people in the life, death, and resurrection of Jesus Christ. Because of Christ, to Rahner, we know that the world "is predestined to salvation and not to perdition, to life and not to death. God no longer waits for the decision of the world. On the contrary, he has spoken the ultimate word as his own Word, and at the same time as that of the world itself. And this word is reconciliation, life, light, victory, and the glory of God himself, which he himself has implanted in the innermost depths of the world itself to become its glory."[26]

Before Christ there was indeed a Spirit but not the Spirit of the Word made flesh. Before the Risen Christ God's Spirit was not present in a visible and irrevocable way. The Spirit as irrevocable gift, the Spirit who definitively reveals God's eternal plan, the invincible Spirit inexorably wedded to the world — "this Spirit was not there before Christ, and since Pentecost it has been revealed that this Spirit is the Spirit of Christ, that in its outpouring and its work in the world it shares in the finality of Christ himself; that it is the Spirit of the crucified and risen Christ, and therefore the Spirit who will no longer disappear from the world and from the community of Christ."[27] Thus, Rahner views the Christ-event as the reason for God's universal and irrevocable self-communication as Holy Spirit, as Love itself, present to all creation.

The Holy Spirit is God's gift of *self* at the core of our being. "That accepted, believed, lived, embraced, and loved in the depths of one's being," Rahner writes, "*that* is the Holy Spirit."[28] The Holy Spirit is the innermost reality of the graced human being. To be a Christian, to Rahner, means to have received God's Spirit, God-in-us, to have been filled with divine life and freedom. The Spirit who searches the depths of God becomes the Spirit of our spirits and searches our depths. This Spirit is not only the mutual communion between God and us, but also our communion with each other. To Rahner, the Spirit is one's unity with God and with other human beings. It is this Spirit whose presence is experienced in the mysticism of everyday life, charismatic mysticism, and the mysticism of the great saints.

The Spirit, to Rahner, has always been the Spirit of Christ because Christ is the very reason the Spirit is given to the world. Always and everywhere — even prior to Jesus Christ —

the experience of God was always an experience of the Spirit of Christ. Rahner also contends that all grace is the grace of Christ, that Christ is present and operative in and through his Spirit even in non-Christians and their religions.

Anonymous Christianity

This grounds Rahner's controversial "anonymous Christian" theory which states that anyone who lives according to conscience does so by the grace of Christ, even if he or she would deny this. This theory offers to *Christians* a way to understand how Christ's grace may operate outside of official Christianity. He never wanted this theory to be used to patronize virtuous non-Christians by telling them that they are in fact Christians without knowing it.

The quotation which follows is illustrative. "Nishitani, the well-known Japanese philosopher, the head of the Kyoto school, who is familiar with the notion of the anonymous Christian, once asked me: 'What would you say to my treating you as an anonymous Zen Buddhist?' I replied: 'Certainly you may and should do so from your point of view; I feel myself honored by such an interpretation, even if I am obliged to regard you as being in error or if I assume that, correctly understood, to be a genuine Zen Buddhist is identical with being a genuine Christian, in the sense directly and properly intended by such statements. Of course in terms of objective social awareness it is indeed clear that the Buddhist is not a Christian and the Christian is not a Buddhist.' Nishitani replied: 'Then on this point we are entirely at one.' "[29] Rahner had also asked Nishitani if the Buddha nature were in everything and if Nishitani found Rahner even a bit enlightened, to which Nishitani had replied yes. According to Nishitani's presuppositions, of course, Rahner is an anonymous Zen Buddhist.

Rahner knows that the Christian view of Jesus Christ, the God-Man, poses one of the greatest difficulties in ecumenical dialogue with the world's great religions. Rahner says that in ecumenical dialogue no side must water down its position. He admits that European theology has traditionally treated Christology before theologizing about the Holy Spirit and grace. "Perhaps an Eastern theology," he writes, "will one day reverse this perspective. Because of God's universal salvific will and in legitimate respect for all the major world religions outside of Christianity, perhaps an Eastern theology will one day make pneumatology, a teaching of the inmost, divinizing gift of grace for all human beings (as an offer to their freedom) the fundamental point of departure for its entire theology, and then attempt from this point — and this is something that might be achieved only with considerable effort — to gain a real and radical understanding of Christology."[30] Thus, for the sake of genuine dialogue with the non-Christian religions of the world, Rahner suggests tentatively that one begin with the Holy Spirit and the primordial experience of God and from this perspective come to a deeper understanding of Jesus Christ.

Love for Jesus Christ

Passionate love of the person of Jesus Christ, says Rahner, must stamp every Christian's life.[31] This seemingly self-evident statement is in fact not so self-evident because to Rahner words such as "love," "life," "fidelity," "truth," and the like are ultimately understood only by being lived. Moreover, since these words are in the final analysis religious words, they ultimately denote God's mystery. These words comprehend us and our lives and become false when their meaning is crystal-clear.

Because human persons are by nature social and made to love and to be loved, they do not really mature until they commit and entrust themselves to others. Rahner notes, however, that a reasonable and responsible self-abandonment to another person requires evidence for so doing. However, the act of entrusting ourselves to others has a radical, absolute, and unconditional quality which is by no means adequately based on sufficient evidence. In other words, "one ventures more, and must venture more, than these grounds seem to justify."[32]

Rahner knows, of course, how much research and scholarship — which he deems necessary and good — have gone into questions about Jesus. He also realizes how many scholarly issues remain unresolved. "But always there remains," he writes, "that 'plus' on the side of freedom to take a risk — on the side of love — precisely — in a truly Christian relationship to Jesus; for this relationship is above and beyond all these historical, exegetical and critical sciences (and of course also above and beyond the historical witness of tradition and the Church concerning Jesus). Only when Jesus himself is accepted and loved in himself, over and above one's own knowledge about him — Jesus himself, and not our mere idea of Christ, nor our mere willingness to brook the lucubrations of historical science — only then does a true relationship to him, the relationship of an absolute self-abandonment to him, begin."[33]

How can we love someone who lived two thousand years ago? Because God is the God of the living, the departed are always really near to us in silent love, a love that transcends space and time. In fact, Rahner maintains that people who have no cult heroes — especially the secular giants of the past — suffer a stunted, diminished humanity. They show no ability to let the heroes of history into their lives, no capacity for dialogue with real past figures. However, genuine love of Jesus Christ requires more than believing that he is now somehow alive in God. This love must be more than hero worship.

The real obstacle that love faces, to Rahner, is not space and time, because lovers do love each other across space and time. Rahner sees the real challenge and mystery of love in the reality of two truly becoming one, yet remaining two. Genuine love must surrender to and affirm the other *as* other. Lovers do successfully meet this challenge. "Hence," Rahner says, "one can love Jesus, love him in himself, in true, genuine, immediate love."[34]

The ultimate reason we can love Jesus Christ is that his life and death became definitive in his resurrection. He is the Risen One. Thus we should read his "biography," the Holy Scriptures, "in the way two lovers gaze at one another in the living of their daily life together."[35] In this way "Jesus becomes, in this love of ours for him, the flesh-and-blood Absolute whom the abstractness of norms and the insignificance of the purely contingent individual are transcended and overcome."[36] Rahner insists that we can and must love Jesus immediately and concretely because the nature of love in general and the power of the Holy Spirit transcend space and time.

In a conversation with a somewhat rationalistic theologian, Rahner said: "You see, you're actually only really dealing with Jesus when you throw your arms around him and realize right down to the bottom of your being that this is something you can still do today."[37] The Risen Christ, to Rahner, did not disappear into God's incomprehensibility. We can and must love this real historical person, the person he is, "on condition that we want to love him, that we have the courage to throw our arms around him."[38]

Precisely who is this Jesus whom we love? Rahner appeals to the significance and force of the Church's two-thousand-year-old faith-interpretation of Jesus' own self-understanding. "Thus the vitality of faith in Jesus down through two millennia is itself a consideration for faith today."[39] Rahner knows that Jesus understands himself to be the Messiah. "He is convinced," Rahner writes, "that with himself the definitive, unsurpassable Kingdom of God has arrived — and in him God shares himself and communicates his own glory and excellence, consoling a sinful world with his irrevocable pardon, speaking his last definitive Word, after which there shall be no other — and that this Word is indeed God himself, in his own excellence."[40] The Messiah, therefore, must be the person in and through whom God's irrevocable Kingdom has come, for the Kingdom of God *is* God himself. The Messiah, to Rahner, must be the Son of God, the very Word of God made flesh.

Only because God has communicated and shared himself in our innermost center are we able to love Jesus in the fullness of his humanity. Rahner notes that human beings want to love unconditionally; however, their love always harbors a secret reservation. How can sinful, finite creatures love unconditionally and absolutely? Every person lives a "searching Christology" insofar as every person seeks an unconditional and absolute love. Thus, one searches for a person who in his human reality can be loved with the absoluteness of God. Only Jesus of Nazareth can be loved without reservations because "in Jesus [our love] knows the Ground of this unconditionality to be given in indissoluble conjunction with him: the God of faithfulness, his own unconditionality."[41]

Love of Jesus Christ, therefore, has the same unconditionality that a person's love for God has. Jesus' unique hypostatic union with God enables us to love this God-Man without hesitation or reservations. This man Jesus fulfills the immense longing contained in a searching Christology.

Love for Jesus Christ and love for neighbor, to Rahner, can never be in competition. We must love our neighbor whom we can see, if we are to love Jesus whom we cannot. These two loves, moreover, mutually strengthen each other. We must love our neighbor in order to be able to love Jesus. However, "it is only in a loving relationship with Jesus that we can conceive the possibilities of love for neighbor that otherwise we should simply not hold feasible, but which present themselves nonetheless whenever we subsume our neighbor in our love for Jesus because he or she is Jesus' brother or sister."[42]

Rahner grants that unconditional love for human beings is possible even for those who have never heard of Christ or for a variety of reasons are not Christians. Yet Rahner does not abandon his Christocentrism even for such cases. "Where love can really abandon all reservations," he writes, "definitely and with absolute assurance, where love can really live out to the last its most proper, most original nature as unconditional self-giving and surrender to the other, there Jesus as such is 'co-loved' as the Ground of this love — even where that blessed Name is as yet altogether unknown to the one who loves. But we Christians can name this primordially and radically loved person. We call him Jesus of Nazareth."[43] Only Jesus of Nazareth guarantees that human love is neither a perversion nor ultimately absurd.

Love for Jesus means more than a merely earthly fulfillment. Love for Jesus is prayer in its deepest sense, that is, the radical act of human existence through which a person surrenders to the incomprehensible God. The person who loves Jesus seeks to share his death through which he surrendered himself totally to God's incomprehensibility and said "Father." The Christian knows that doing so is not absurd. "Indeed, Jesus himself," Rahner writes, "as the Crucified One who rose again, is, on the one hand, the human being who has accomplished this unconditional capitulation to God; and on the other hand, it is in this case alone that we know with the certitude of faith that this capitulation and self surrender has actually been accepted — that the whole of the existence of that person has been given over to God without stint or reserve and that God has accepted and taken up that surrender and that existence. All that comes with faith in Jesus as the Resurrected One."[44]

Devotion to the Sacred Heart

Devotion to the Sacred Heart of Jesus plays an important role in Rahner's spiritual and theological life. His doctoral dissertation focused on patristic understandings of the key biblical text for this devotion: "But one of the soldiers pierced [Christ's] side with a spear, and at once there came out blood and water" (John 19:34). So much did Rahner write on the Sacred Heart that several dissertations and numerous articles have been written about his interpretation.

Only a year before his death he wrote an article in which he lamented the demise of this devotion in the Western world. Agreeing that the Church changes and that the same God-given realities do not always occupy the foreground of Christian faith, Rahner nonetheless maintains that worship of the Sacred Heart of Jesus belongs to the Church's identity. With Pope Pius XII Rahner agrees that in some sense devotion to Christ's Sacred Heart can be called the *summa religionis,* religion's high point.[45] That God's eternal Word who flows eternally from the Father's heart finds, endures, and keeps our hearts for all eternity — this expresses the whole meaning of Christian existence. Thus Rahner writes, "I intend to defend the position that even today the worship of the divine heart of Jesus Christ can and should be meaningful and significant."[46]

Rahner looks at the incredible complexity and variety in the Church's two-thousand-year history of living and reflecting upon the one mystery of God's triune love for us in Christ. Christianity's simple nature has developed an almost bewildering array of devotions and religious practices, an impressive sacramental system, numerous doctrines, and manifold ways of living a Christian life. The Christian, to Rahner, is not allowed to choose only what suits the needs of the moment and to let the rest go by the board. Nor is a Christian capable of achieving a view that somehow comprehends it all. Yet again and again in the Church's life there flames up a mystical longing for an ultimate unity in which all the different forms of Christian living and all complexities are done away with and resolved in a dark, mysterious mysticism in which there are no "ways." To Rahner, devotion to Jesus' Sacred Heart speaks to this longing because this heart is the reality by which

God's ineffable mystery gives itself to — and fills — our human mystery.

"Heart," to Rahner, is a primordial word — a word which grasps us before we grasp it. Linked with the mystery of human existence, "heart" expresses the center of our being, our interiority, the innermost unity from which and back into which our daily lives must flow. It is the point at which the mystery of a human being passes into God's mystery. "The infinite emptiness which lies at the innermost center of man," Rahner writes, "cries out to be filled with the infinite fullness of God. The heart that is adjured in this word is the heart that has been pierced, weighed down by angst, drained to its last drop, overcome by death. What is designated in this word is that which signifies a love which is selfless and beyond all conception, the love which is victorious in failure, which triumphs when it has been deprived of its power, raises to life when it has been slain. It is the love that is God."[47]

When Rahner ponders the injustices, brutality, futility, guilt, and death which permeate human evolution, he speaks of a "sewer of world history and human history"[48] in which all hope should drown. "And when we experience all this," Rahner says, "then let us look to the Sacred Heart pierced by the lance and say to ourselves: 'The basis of all reality is love.' Let us say to ourselves: 'It is from this source alone that there streams out also this incomprehensible reality with its multiplicity, its contradictions, its agonies, its endless journeys to unknown goals, together with its blind alleys, its struggles and deaths, its darkness, its total incomprehensibility.' "[49]

Thus, this anguished, often loveless and absurd world has in fact pierced the divine-human heart of the eternal Logos who springs eternally from the Father's heart. "Only if we direct our gaze to the heart of Christ," Rahner writes, "do we know what love is: the mystery of the world, the overcoming of the terrors which are in the world, that which unifies and embraces us, that which transforms, that which liberates and is tender, that which is realized only in its fullness when the one who loves makes a total surrender of everything pertaining to the movement of his own personal history towards its fulfillment. This is achieved when this love of his is pierced through and silently pours out his heart's blood into the futility of the world, and thereby conquers it."[50]

To Rahner, then, "when we say 'heart of Jesus' we evoke the innermost core of Jesus Christ, and we say that it is filled with the mystery of God. We say...in a way that contradicts all our experiences of emptiness, futility, and death, that there reigns in this heart the infinite love of God's self-giving.... The heart that was pierced, that loves us in the darkness of our hopeless-ness, that is God's very heart and that, without abolishing it, discloses to us God's fundamental mystery....

"We look at the heart of the Lord and the question that is decisive for eternity fills our innermost being, our innermost heart and life: Do you love me? Do you love me in such a way that this love generates a blessed eternity, that it truly, power-fully, and invincibly generates my everlasting life?...But when [this question] enters this heart, because it is asked with faith, hope, and love, this question is not answered but overpowered by the mystery that is love, by the unquestionable reality of the mystery of God.... We must eventually, in the luminous and in the dark hours of life, try to pray: 'Heart of Jesus, have mercy on us....' We might venture to use this word like a mantra in Eastern style meditation. But over and above all that, we must experience in life that it is most improbable, most impos-sible, and so most evident that God, the incomprehensible, truly loves us and that in the heart of Jesus this love has become irrevocable."[51]

Conclusion

The following words, which Rahner puts into the mouth of St. Ignatius of Loyola, offer an excellent summary of Rahner's approach to Christ:

"But now I must speak about Jesus. Did what I say before sound as if I had forgotten Jesus and his blessed Name? I have not forgotten him. He was intimately present in everything I said before, even if the words I addressed to you...could not say everything at once. I say *Jesus*....

"I admit gladly that in my case you can find many exam-ples of a medieval devotion to the man Jesus.... But why should I fret if people do not find this devotion particularly original? Is it so obsolete? Is it something which today cannot be understood at all? Does not this medieval devotion to Jesus the man contain in itself the possibility of fulfilling what your contemporary emphasis on Jesus the man seeks? Instead of comprehending that God has expressed and promised Himself precisely in this man as such, do you not presuppose instead that you can find Jesus the man only if you pompously and simplistically pronounce God dead?

"I never had a problem — or at most the one of loving and being a true disciple — finding in a unique way God in Jesus and Jesus in God. And I mean Jesus as he really and truly is in flesh and blood, such that love alone — not hairsplitting reason — can say in what way he should be imitated if one is his disciple. It is from being able to narrate Jesus' story that one has then narrated the history of the eternal, incomprehensible God, without dissolving this history into theory. Moreover, this history must always be narrated anew, and therein Jesus' and God's own history continues to unfold.

"Since my conversion I knew Jesus to be God's unconditional loving condescension to the world and to me, the love in which the incomprehensibility of pure mystery is totally present and through which a person attains his or her perfection. Jesus' singularity, the necessity of seeking him in a limited treasury of events and words with the intention of finding in this limited reality the infinite and ineffable mystery — this never bothered me....

"There is no Christianity which can bypass Jesus to find the incomprehensible God. God has willed that legions find Him because they seek Jesus — even though they do not know Jesus' Name, and even though they plunge into death sharing with Jesus the experience of abandonment by God without benefit of knowing how to name this fate or how to name the One with whom they share it. God has permitted this darkness of finitude and guilt in the world only because God has made it his own in Jesus.

"This Jesus I thought about, loved, and desired to follow. And this was the way in which I found the real, living God without having made Him a figment of my own unbridled speculation. A person gets beyond such speculation only by dying a real death throughout life. But this death is real only if the person, resigned with Jesus, accepts in it the abandonment by God. This is the ultimate 'wayless' mysticism. In so speaking I know that I have not clarified the mystery of the unity of history and God. But it is in Jesus who surrendered to God in his crucifixion and received God in his resurrection that this unity is definitively present. It is in Jesus that this unity can be accepted in faith, hope, and love."[52]

Notes

1. *Karl Rahner in Dialogue,* 196.
2. "The Two Basic Types of Christology," *TI XIII,* 215–16.
3. *Spiritual Exercises,* 123.
4. Ibid., 121.
5. "The Two Basic Types of Christology," *TI XIII,* 215–16.
6. For the sources of the remarks which follow, see "Remarks on the Dogmatic Treatise 'De Trinitate'" and "On the Theology of the Incarnation," *TI IV,* 77–102, 105–20. Also see *Foundations of Christian Faith,* 212–27. An excellent summary of Rahner's descending Christology can be found in "The Two Basic Types of Christology," *TI XIII,* 217–19.
7. "On the Theology of the Incarnation," *TI IV,* 109–10.
8. Ibid., 116.
9. Ibid., 119.
10. "Death," *Encyclopedia of Theology,* 332.
11. Ibid., 332.
12. "Christology in a Evolutionary View," *TI V,* 185.
13. See ibid., 157–92.
14. "On the Theology of the Incarnation," *TI IV,* 119.
15. "The Christian Understanding of Redemption," *TI XXI,* trans. Hugh M. Riley (New York: Crossroad Publishing Co., 1988), 249. In this same volume, also see "Reconciliation and Vicarious Representation," 255–69.
16. *Foundations of Christian Faith,* 284.
17. For the sources of the remarks which follow, see "On the Spirituality of the Easter Faith" and "Jesus' Resurrection," *TI XVII,* 8–15 and 16–23.
18. "On the Spirituality of the Easter Faith," *TI XVII,* 14.
19. See, for example, "Remarks on the Importance of the History of Jesus for Catholic Dogmatics," *TI XIII,* 201–12.
20. "On the Spirituality of the Easter Faith," *TI XVII,* 13.
21. "A Faith That Loves the Earth," *Everyday Faith,* 80–81.

22. "Jesus' Resurrection," *TI XVII*, 18–19.

23. Ibid., 19.

24. "Remarks on the Importance of the History of Jesus for Catholic Dogmatics," *TI XIII*, 202. My emphasis.

25. For the sources for the remarks which follow, see "The Holy Spirit as the Fruit of Redemption," *Spiritual Exercises*, 251–56; "The Church as the Subject of the Sending of the Spirit" and "The Spirit That Is over All Life," *TI VII*, 186–92 and 193–201.

26. "The Spirit That Is over All Life," *TI VII*, 197.

27. Ibid., 197.

28. "The Holy Spirit as the Fruit of Redemption," *Spiritual Exercises*, 252.

29. "The One Christ and the Universality of Salvation," *TI XVI*, 219.

30. "Aspects of European Theology," *TI XXI*, 97–98. Translation emended.

31. For the source of the remarks which follow, see "What Does It Mean to Love Jesus?" *The Love of Jesus and the Love of Neighbor*, 11–46.

32. Ibid., 17.

33. Ibid., 18.

34. Ibid., 22.

35. Ibid.

36. Ibid., 23.

37. Ibid.

38. Ibid.

39. Ibid., 26.

40. Ibid., 27.

41. Ibid., 41.

42. Ibid., 23–24.

43. Ibid., 44.

44. Ibid., 45.

45. See "The Theological Meaning of the Veneration of the Sacred Heart" and "Unity — Love — Mystery," *TI VIII*, 217–28 and 229–47.

46. "Devotion to the Sacred Heart Today," *TI XXIII*, 117.

47. "The Theological Meaning of the Veneration of the Sacred Heart," *TI VIII*, 222.

48. Ibid., 237.

49. "Unity — Love — Mystery," *TI VIII*, 237.

50. Ibid., 239–40.

51. "Devotion to the Sacred Heart Today," *TI XXIII*, 126–28.

52. "Rede des Ignatius von Loyola," *Schriften zur Theologie XV*, 384–86. For an alternate translation, see "Ignatius of Loyola Speaks to a Modern Jesuit," *Ignatius of Loyola*, 19–21.

Chapter 7

Karl Rahner — Teacher of Church and Sacraments

The average books on the Church and its sacraments often approach these themes extrinsically. They fail to show the inner connection between God's universal self-communicating love (grace) and how this love has a long history. They also neglect to show how this genuine salvation history relates to the human person as an individual, social, and historical being.

The traditional theology states that after Adam and Eve sinned, God withdrew his self-communicating love until the Son was sent to redeem us by dying on the cross. It likewise understands a significant aspect of Christ's redemptive work in his founding of the institutional Church. According to this view, the link between Christ and his Church is understood almost legalistically. So too with the traditional view of the relationship between the Church and its sacraments.

In contrast, Rahner's understanding of the Church and its sacraments begins with God's universal self-communication to the world and to the interior of every human being — even prior to the Christ event. God's self-communicating love has a history in which God's grace is mediated, embodied, celebrated, and eventually brought to its full expression in Jesus Christ. To Rahner, the Church flows from Christ's very nature. The Church is Christ's historical-social Body which must express itself sacramentally to be itself. One of the most precious gifts from Rahner's spiritual legacy is his universal, cosmic view which inexorably relates God's self-communicating love to world religions, the person of Jesus Christ, his Church, and the Church's sacraments.

Grace as God's Self-Communication

Rahner never ceases to emphasize that "the world is permeated by the grace of God.... The world is constantly and ceaselessly possessed by grace from its innermost roots, from the innermost center of the spiritual subject."[1] He rejects an older, yet still operative, theological opinion which thinks of God's grace primarily as interventions in the world at discrete points in space and time. This notion tacitly assumes that God's very own self-communication can be a totally unmerited gift only if God gives it sporadically — and in a secular and sinful world otherwise deprived of it.

In contrast, Rahner understands grace as gushing from the innermost heart and center of the human being and of the entire world. God's self-communication, to Rahner, "does not take place as a special phenomenon, as one particular process apart from the rest of human life. Rather it is quite simply the ultimate depths and the radical dimension of all that which the spiritual person experiences, achieves, and suffers in all those areas in which he achieves his own fullness, and so in his laughter and his tears, in his taking of responsibility, in his loving, living, and dying, whenever he keeps faith with the truth, breaks through his own egotism in his relationships with his neighbor, whenever he hopes against all hope, whenever he smiles and refuses to be disquieted or embittered by the folly of his everyday pursuits, whenever he is able to be silent, and whenever within this silence of the heart that evil which a man has engendered against another in his heart does not develop any further into external action, but rather dies within this heart as its grave — whenever, in a word, life is lived as a man would seek to live it, in such a way as to overcome his own egotism and the despair of the heart which constantly assails him. *There* grace has the force of an event, because all this of its very nature ... loses itself in God's silent infinity, is hidden in his absolute unconditionality in the future of the fullness of victory which in turn is God himself."[2]

Grace as the heart of everyday life was *always* present and active in the world, in the depths of every human being, even prior to the life, death, and resurrection of Jesus Christ. In fact, Rahner considers God's self-communication as the animating force in the entire evolutionary process and world history. The history of salvation, to Rahner, is therefore coextensive, but not identical, with the whole of world history. Whenever and wherever human beings interpret themselves in art, litera- ture, society, technology, and the like, the divine-human drama unfolds itself as the hidden leaven in human culture.

Because human beings are social, historical, traditional, and religious creatures, they must translate and express in space and time the divine-human congress in the depths of their hearts. Even the most depraved religion, to Rahner, success- fully awakens to some extent the mysticism of everyday life dormant in the human heart. The great religions of the world are the more or less successful interpretations and expressions of this mysticism of everyday life. No religion, to Rahner, lacks the grace of God, no religion is unimportant for a per- son's salvation. Nonetheless, he views every religion but one as a somewhat skewed and inadequate interpretation of the divine-human drama.

How does a Christian know that God's grace has conquered the human heart and has been irrevocably accepted? Because the divine-human drama — that is, the history of God's self- communication and its free human acceptance — attains its full flowering in the crucified and risen Christ. To Rahner, "this innermost dynamism of the normal 'profane' life of man as it exists always and everywhere has found in Jesus of Nazareth its clearest manifestation, and in him has proved itself as real, vic- torious, and arriving at God. And it has done this precisely in a life of this kind, in which he has become like us in all things, in other words in a life which is completely everyday in charac- ter, a life bound up with birth, toil, courage, hope, failure, and death."[3] Jesus Christ, crucified and risen, is the norm against which Rahner measures all the religions of the world.

Jesus' death is the perfect expression of unreserved surren- der to God's self-offer, the supreme act of adoring God and God alone. His resurrection gives proof of the Father's acceptance and confirmation of Jesus' self-interpretation, his life of total self-surrender to the Father's will. The resurrection validates the Christian claim that dying to self and to all created things is not ultimately absurd because God will "one day reveal him- self even to the pure mystic as the God of the transfigured earth because he [the mystic] is more than pure spirit."[4] In Jesus Christ one finds the criterion for measuring all other religions because what is expressed (God's Word) and the mode of expression (Jesus in his human reality) are made absolutely one. Thus, Christ is *the* sacrament of everyday life, the incarnation of God's irrevocable and efficacious offer of self to the world.

The Church of Jesus Christ and His Spirit

God's victorious and irrevocable self-communication to the world takes place in the crucified and risen Christ, whom Rahner calls the absolute mediator of salvation. "The historical continuation of Christ, in and through the community of those who believe in him, and who recognize him explicitly as the mediator of salvation in a profession of faith," Rahner maintains, "is what we call Church."[5] The Church is the historically and institutionally tangible continuation of the Christ-event. It is the Body of Christ.

"In Jesus of Nazareth," Rahner writes, "we have the living God of the living Spirit and of grace. The Church is nothing else than the further projection of the historicity and of the visibility of Jesus through space and time, and every word of her message, every one of her sacramental signs, is, once more, nothing else than a part of the world in its earthiness, with which the Spirit has united itself indissolubly since the day on which the Logos became flesh."[6]

The Church is the concreteness of Jesus Christ and his Spirit, thus the absolute Church. The salvation history of God's grace reached its climax in the Church of the absolute savior. Suffused with Christ's Spirit — God's victorious communication of self as love to the depths of our being and to all reality — this Church thus possesses the authority of the Spirit of truth. It is not constituted by our whims and religious needs, but challenges us, and often stands against our subjectivity. It is certainly not the loudspeaker of public opinion.

An Indiscussible Relationship to the Church

Rahner's understanding of Jesus Christ and of his Spirit grounds his indiscussible relationship to the Church. When asked by an interviewer to "define Karl Rahner," he replied: "I am a Catholic theologian who attempts, in absolute loyalty to the magisterium of the Church, to rethink Catholic teaching."[7] More than one person has marveled at Rahner's "indiscussible relationship to the Church."[8] Because he considers such a relationship to be an essential component in every Catholic's believing, hoping, and loving relationship to God himself, he finds it odd that his own attitude edifies people.

Within this absolute relationship to the Church, of course, many difficulties may arise. All conflicts and troubles, however, remain secondary because they occur within an ultimately positive relationship to the Church, just as they do in an indissoluble marriage. "The Church itself," he says, "must be affirmed as an inner, necessary, and valid moment in my Christian faith.... When I affirm that, in what in the strict sense is called 'Church,' I hear in a believable way the absolute promise of God in which he says to me in Jesus Christ, crucified and risen, 'In the absolute power of my love I communicate myself to you and that for all eternity,' then measured by that everything else is secondary."[9]

Rahner's indiscussible relationship to the Church is part of his enormous spiritual legacy. He took a certain pride in being called a man of the Church. The following words he put into the mouth of St. Ignatius of Loyola came from Rahner's heart and also reveal his own attitude toward the Church: "Participating in God's deference to the concrete Body of his Son in history I loved the Church, and in this mystical union of God with the Church — granted the radical difference between the two — the Church was and remained a transparent view towards God for me and the concrete place of my ineffable relationship to the eternal Mystery. There is the source of my disposition towards the Church, my participation in the sacramental life, my fidelity to the papacy, and the ecclesial nature of my mission to help souls."[10]

Thus the question of some disgruntled Catholics — "Shall I still remain in the Church?" — Rahner dismisses as "meaningless chatter which turns my stomach."[11] Only a few weeks before his death Rahner told an interviewer: "I am not in the Church to feel comfortable, but only because in it Jesus' call is perceived. Still, that doesn't change the fact that I have reservations about the concrete shape of this Church, or that, if necessary, I might even express my critical reservations openly."[12]

Around this same time period he said to another interviewer: "If I have the time and energy, I would still like to write a small book in Herder's paperback collection called 'Why I Am a Catholic.' This isn't the same question as 'Why I am a Christian.' Despite all my ecumenical openness and willingness to be reconciled, the fact remains that I must be and want to be a Catholic, a Roman Catholic. This decision is not optional, as, for example, deciding to buy things in one store rather than in another. Even today I consider religious indifference as something completely erroneous, despite my conviction that the Christian confessions can and must do more than what they have done to unite in the one Church of Christ."[13]

The Church as Community

Rahner rejects as a late bourgeois conception the notion that religion is a private matter. The human person is not only an individual but also a social being. The whole person in all the dimensions of his or her life must be orientated to God. Faith, therefore, must assume not only a private, interior form but must also express itself historically and socially. If love of neighbor is love of God, then both loves must have something to do with society and Church.

To an interviewer who stated that one does not necessarily need to belong to an institutional Church to fulfill Christianity's most important concern, love of neighbor, Rahner replied: "I believe that the most magnificent and radical act of love of neighbor is not simply to provide food and clothing but rather to be concerned about the absolute and incomprehensible God taking this person into his own inner life; if, in other words, I consider the bringing of the good news the highest act of human love, then it is obvious how such a broad notion of love of neighbor automatically leads into the realm of the Church."[14]

With that, Rahner refuses to reduce human existence and all human needs to the things of this world. He does indeed insist though that genuine love of neighbor must also be practical, that is, worldly. While praising the good work of the Salvation

Army and other such groups, Rahner nevertheless contends that Christianity must also concern itself with initiating people into a life of genuine faith, hope, and love — the life of God himself.

Contemporary trends — especially among the young — seem in Rahner's view to eschew old-fashioned individualism to embrace community, social structures which foster intimacy, service to one's neighbor, and the like. The growing number of cults and sects seem to be evidence of the contemporary thirst for new communal ways of living. Rahner therefore finds it ironic when people shout: "Christ, yes; the Church, no." Genuine community, to Rahner, "is always something other than, or more than, an arbitrary sympathy group of a few young people that soon disintegrates again. And I would really like to know how long today's young sects will last. Without a doubt they arouse a certain feeling of protection and a strong emotionality. They will very quickly fall apart. . . . I do not deny, however, that the Church often in its mission makes obstacles for itself which could be avoided. Still, you have to say that in the sociality of a genuine community of faith certain demands arise automatically; sacrifice and renunciation are expected. And for this reason, for example, I can grant completely to a bishop or a pope that he has a normative, limited, and correctly defined significance for my religious life, even if right now I might not care for him that much personally."[15] If a community is to be an enduring foundation of one's life, discipline and community structures are necessary. One cannot enjoy the blessings of family life, for example, unless one is willing to give as well as to receive.

Genuine God-given human faith forms community, has a history, and professes itself both privately and publicly. Therefore, to Rahner, Christianity is necessarily ecclesial. In line with an ancient tradition Rahner avers that one cannot have God as one's Father and Jesus as one's Brother, unless one also has the Church as one's Mother. "If the comparison between the relation of a Christian to the Church and that of a child to its parents still bothers you," Rahner says, "then disregard it. Ecclesial language often refers to 'Mother Church.' It is a custom that goes back to earliest Christianity. What it affirms is something that really makes sense: the Church is the mediator and guarantor of my life in unity and solidarity with God. To this degree I can call the Church my mother."[16]

Church, Churches, and World Religions

Rahner insists, of course, that Jesus himself founded the Church, and not vice versa. The latest exegetical studies bolster Rahner's claim that "there is one Church which was founded by Christ and was won by Christ and is united with Christ. It is at the same time a visible and an invisible Church, it has an earthly and a heavenly mode of existence, and it possesses both an exterior form and an interior, Spirit-filled and mysterious essence."[17]

Because Jesus, too, is social by nature, he cannot be himself without community. He did not merely address individuals in the interiority of their consciences. His call and its salvific significance build Church. Because Jesus is the absolute savior, at least some people must necessarily come to believe in him — and this without prejudice to individual human freedom. Therefore, as God's victorious and irrevocable self-offer to the world, Jesus must evoke abiding, indefectible faith. The Church, to Rahner, springs from Jesus' essence and is as essential a part of Christianity as the very event of salvation.

Yet Rahner eschews any type of militant Christianity which makes the Church the focal point of Christian existence. It is not Christianity's central reality. "Jesus Christ, faith and love, entrusting oneself to the darkness of existence and into the incomprehensibility of God in trust and in the company of Jesus Christ, the crucified and risen one," Rahner states, "these are the central realities for a Christian."[18]

The Christian also knows that God always and everywhere offers himself to the very depths of human freedom. Thus there are good grounds for believing that even agnostics and atheists may implicitly accept this offer. "For wherever a person," Rahner says, "accepts his existence ultimately and unconditionally, and an ultimate trust that it can be accepted, and wherever a person allows himself to fall into the abyss of the mystery of his existence with ultimate resolve and ultimate trust, he is accepting God."[19] Rahner thus agrees with St. Augustine that the

Church may have some whom God does not have and that God may have some whom the Church does not have.

On the other hand, the full, historical, and social actualization of God's self-communication in Christ is found in the Church. "Before the incarnation of the Logos," Rahner writes, "the invisible [Holy Spirit] was not present in a mode that was visible and *lasting*....In the fullness of time, a visible mode... has actually been achieved, in the incarnate Logos and in his Body the Church....These are the words of Irenaeus: 'Where the Church is, there is the Spirit of God; and where the Spirit of God is, there is the Church and every grace....God ordained that the entire work of the Spirit should take place in the Church.' And where the Spirit is active, there, at any rate remotely, a stage is achieved in the construction of the visible body of the Church. Thus for Catholics the life of the Spirit, wherever it occurs, is always included within the fold of the Church. And everything else is not the life of the Holy Spirit but rather mere religious excitement. There is no Holy Spirit without the holy Body that is the Church. For this reason we are 'spiritualized,' that is, those possessed and permeated by the Holy Spirit, those acting in and through the Holy Spirit, only if we are incorporated in the Body of the Church."[20]

As the historical, social visibility of God's irreversible, victorious self-communication in Christ and his Spirit, Christianity is not simply one among many world religions. Rahner therefore rejects the relativistic position that one religion is just as good as another. On the other hand, he affirms that Christ's Spirit is operative in them and that they are conducive to salvation. "Now Christianity," Rahner says, "cannot let go of the claim both to have received the definitive and all-embracing word of grace in Jesus, crucified and risen, and to preach this still to the world today. But this is not to deny that the liberating Spirit of God is active in all finite human affairs, within every perplexity and error. The non-Christian world religions witness in their own fashion not only to human limitation but also to the Spirit of Jesus. Certainly many of their major experiences can provisionally be included in the comprehensive answer of Jesus, because the history of the Christian message is far from complete."[21] Thus even "anonymous Christians," to Rahner, do belong to the Church, "the Church who is the promise of salvation even for that world which has not yet recognized itself explicitly as a part of the Church."[22]

Rahner also finds the Church of Christ in the Catholic Church "because according to the very simple evidence it possesses in the concrete a closer, more evident and less encumbered historical continuity with the Church of the past going all the way back to apostolic times.... The Catholic Church is a church in which there is a Petrine office and an episcopacy which have an evident historical connection with the Church going all the way back to apostolic times."[23] The Catholic Church, therefore, is the institution which evinces the closest possible historical continuity and proximity to original Christianity.

Although Catholics cannot recognize in Protestant Churches the same salvific and theological quality with respect to the question of the Church of Jesus Christ, Rahner would in no way deny their positive significance both for their members and for the Catholic Church. The contemporary Catholic Church owes much to the existence of the Protestant Churches. In fact, there is more that unites than separates the Churches. "I believe," Rahner says, "that if Rome were to be as tolerant in regard to the non-Catholic Churches of the West as it is in regard to the Oriental Churches, a catholic unity would indeed be possible. Obviously Rome would have to restrain its continuing tendency to centralization and uniformity. In this case of unity with Protestants, Rome ought not to demand more in regard to orthodoxy and the unity of faith than what is demanded in practice of individual believers within the Catholic Church itself."[24]

The Sinful Church

Rahner stresses too that the one, holy Church is also sinful because we her members are sinful. This sinfulness comprises more than the sum total of the private sins of her members, including those who bear her highest and most sacred offices. The sinfulness of her members has its effects also in the actions and conduct which must be designated as the actions and conduct of the Church herself. "The Church is a sinful Church," Rahner states. "This is a truth of faith, not an elementary fact of experience.... When the Church acts, gives a lead, makes decisions (or fails to make decisions when they ought to be made), when she proclaims her message, and when she is obliged to proclaim it in accordance with the times and historical situations, this activity of the Church is not carried out by some abstract principle and not by the Holy Spirit alone, but rather this whole activity of the Church is at the same time the activity of concrete men."[25]

Rahner rejects the thesis which concedes that there are sinners in the Church but that they have nothing to do with the "real Church." Only the concrete Church is the Church. Again and again, Rahner rejects any idealized or spiritualized view of the Church. We must give our yes or no to the actually existing Church. Therefore, Rahner would have us examine our own egotism, mediocrity, and cowardice before daring to cast the first stone at the "official" Church. *We are* the holy and sinful Church.

Rahner knows that where sin abounds, grace abounds all the more. Because of God's victorious and irreversible self-communication in the crucified and risen Christ, we know that God's forgiveness, healing, and life have the last word. The Gospels never portray Christ and Satan as equals. So, "if holiness and sin coexist in the 'image' presented by the Church (and the Church is essentially 'image,' a sign making historically accessible the grace of God in the world)," Rahner writes, "this is of course not to say that sin and holiness have the same relationship to the hidden essential purpose of the Church and therefore belong to her in the same way. The holiness made tangible in her history is an expression of what she is and will remain infallibly and indestructibly until the end of time: the presence in the world of God and of his grace.... On the other hand, the sin in the appearance of the Church is indeed really in the Church herself insofar as she is essentially 'body' and a historical structure and insofar as in this dimension there can be sin.... But this sin in the Church is not a revelation of what the Church is in her own, proper, living roots, but on the contrary a veiling of it from view; it is in a way an exogenetic illness in the bodily nature of the Church, not an endogenetic hereditary flaw in the Church herself (even though sin always betrays 'what is in man')."[26]

The Church as Sacrament of the World's Salvation

As the community of the crucified and risen Christ, the Church is the sacrament of the world's salvation. To Rahner, the "Church, as the socially constituted presence of Christ in every age up to the end, can therefore rightly be called the basic sacrament of mankind. By this we mean that it is the sign which perpetuates Christ's presence in the world, the permanent and unsurpassable sign that the gracious entelechy of the whole of history, which brings this history into God Himself, will really be victorious in the world despite all sin and darkness and will really prevail by bringing about the completion of the world in the form of salvation rather than judgment."[27] For this reason the Church, to Rahner, is either "the explicit or also anonymous soul of the world."[28]

The Church is the sacrament of the world's salvation not only through her explicit preaching of the Gospel and her sacramental life but also by way of everything her members do and suffer. The very Spirit of Christ becomes visibly embodied at the historical and social level through the graced actions and sufferings of the members of the Church. "But wherever and however the Church is this ultimate sacrament of salvation for the world," Rahner writes, "there Christ is present in his Spirit, and there he makes this presence of his palpable also, even though it may be in a way that is 'anonymous.' It is because of this that the Lord himself says that he is present, though unrecognized, wherever one man shows compassion from his heart to another."[29]

To be herself as the soul of the world the Church must preach, administer the sacraments, and act upon and in history. The Church cannot confine herself to the sacral dimension of life. Wherever genuine social work — practical acts of charity — requires faith, hope, and love in order to be sustained over the long run, the Church has the right and the duty to engage in such activity.

The Sacraments of the Church

The Church, to Rahner, is the social-historical continuation of the Christ-event, the visibility of Christ's Spirit, the efficacious sign that God's self-offer and its acceptance have been made one by God. When the Church as the sacrament of the world's salvation utters her word of grace, makes it more comprehensible through symbolic gesture, and pledges the truth of her whole existence, she re-presents the historical presence of God. When she addresses this word to an individual at the significant moments of his or her life, she utters and performs a sacrament. This irrevocable word of God's grace not only speaks of grace but gives it visible form in space and time.

Were a Christian to understand the Church's sacraments as a demarcated enclave in which there and only there is God present and God's grace operative, then he or she would tragically misunderstand the universal experience of God's grace — the mysticism of everyday life. To Rahner, the Church's sacraments are "the necessary, meaningful, indispensable, small signs in the vastness of the God-saturated world that remind us of the boundless presence of God's grace, and in this way, and [by] this anamnesis alone, become an event of grace."[30]

The Church's sacraments are intrinsically linked to the mysticism of everyday life, which in a different context Rahner calls the "liturgy of the world" and the "sacraments of everyday life."[31] The Church's official sacraments awaken, deepen, strengthen, and bring to full expression the sacraments of everyday life. As the acts by which Christ's eschatological community engages its whole being and expresses itself as the sacrament of the world's salvation at decisive moments in a person's history, they incarnate and bring to full flowering the sacraments of everyday life.

"When the will of God towards the world as forgiving it and permeating it with his own divinity," Rahner writes, "is explicitly proclaimed in this Church in the word of preaching, in the creed, in the sacral sign, then, while this proclamation is certainly effective, what it proclaims is not a saving event which takes place only in the explicitly sacral sphere of the proclamation itself. What this proclamation constitutes rather is an explicit revelation of a saving will on God's part which is addressed in the form of judgment and grace to the whole world in all its dimensions and epochs, and which can still achieve victory even in those spheres in which it is never accepted at all at the level of conscious and explicit decision. For

the acceptance can take a purely anonymous form and consist simply in maintaining integrity and honesty throughout
the vicissitudes of life. From this point of view alone, then,
the Church as a whole is not simply identical with the salvation of the world. Rather she constitutes the historical and
symbolic manifestation of this salvation, the basic sacrament of
the world's salvation."[32] In other words both the Church and
her official sacraments make more explicit the often anonymous
experiences of grace at the heart of human existence.

The Seven Sacraments

Eucharist

In speaking of the Church's Eucharist Rahner notes that the
world and its history "are the terrible and sublime liturgy,
breathing of death and sacrifice, which God celebrates and
permits to be celebrated in the free history of humanity, this
history which he in turn sustains in grace through his sovereign disposition. In the entire length and breadth of this
immense history of birth and death, replete with superficial-
ity, folly, inadequacy and hatred (all of which 'crucify') on the
one hand, and silent submission, responsibility unto death in
dying and in joyfulness, in successes and failures on the other
hand, is the true liturgy of the world present. It is present in
such a way that the liturgy which the Son brought to its absolute fulfillment on the cross belongs intrinsically to it, emerges
from it, that is, from the ultimate source of the world's grace,
and constitutes the supreme point of this liturgy from which all
else draws its life, because everything else is always dependent
upon the supreme goal and at the same time sustained by it."[33]

Christians, therefore, should not understand the Eucharist
as a sacral ghetto in the midst of a profane, pagan world.
"The Mass," to Rahner, "should be understood as the explicit
coming-to-awareness of this tremendous drama, full of guilt
and grace, that unfolds in the whole of world history, therefore also in our times and in our life. It assumes a meaning, it
peaks in that death in which Jesus, in the incomprehensibility
of his death, surrendered in total confidence to the mystery of
forgiving love, to the mystery we call God. We do not always

dwell at the core of our incomprehensible being, we stay on the surface, we are exiled to humdrum, bustling everyday life. Yet once in a while, we too are thrown into the mystery of guilt, death, forgiveness, and unfathomable freedom that issues from God into the midst of our life."[34]

Take, for example, a person who endures the crucifixion of everyday life silently and filled with radical hope. This person celebrates the Eucharist of everyday life, which finds its fulfillment in the Church's Eucharist. In other words, when someone goes to Mass, "under the forms of bread and wine he offers the world in that he knows that it itself is already ceaselessly offering itself up in rejoicing, tears, and blood to God's incomprehensibility."[35]

Baptism

If a person comprehends, however anonymously, that God is in love with us and that we are all at least secretly in love with each other; that love is life's meaning; that God has given himself to us even before we freely respond to him and that God enables us to respond freely; that one must say yes with one's entire being to the fullness haunting the depths of our lives — that person has received the baptism of everyday life. Again, the baptism of everyday life flowers fully in the Church's baptism.

"What happens in the baptism of a child?" Rahner asks. "Simply, what is *always* happening for our salvation is here more clearly revealed: God anticipates our need, His mercy enfolds us before we call upon it.... What is done here is a sign and manifestation on the surface of life in order to express the hidden action of God.... God loves this child that is here baptized, but not just from the moment of his baptism. It is because he already loved him that the child, through God's merciful providence, comes to be baptized as the child of a Christian family.... There never was a moment... when this life, this person, and his eternal destiny were not present to Him, enfolded in His all-creative wisdom and embraced in His divine love. From all eternity He has seen this child as someone belonging to His Eternal Word, the Logos.... God wants this life to be lived in time, in history.... It is God's own time, the divine history of salvation and mercy which must unfold here and now.... Therefore it cannot be that everything has already been given by God to this child before he begins to live in time."[36] In other words, the Church's baptism of a child expresses God's eternal will to communicate self to a person. It expresses the victory of God's grace in the crucified and risen Lord. It makes tangible and visible in a social setting God's eternal love for us and the person to be baptized. Baptism also bestows a mandate and a capacity to participate in the Church's function to be the historical tangibility of God's grace in the world.

Confirmation

Let us also consider a person who maintains a single sustaining hope throughout the ups and downs of everyday life; who assumes responsibility with no tangible prospects of success; who endures life's bitterness with a strength from some elusive source; and who entrusts self and everything else to a mystery that far exceeds all personal achievements — this person lives the confirmation of everyday life even before its fulfillment in ecclesial confirmation. Such a person gives witness to the deepest meaning of Christ's sacrifice on the cross: God and God alone confirms a person's deepest identity, that one can trust God, despite appearances to the contrary.

To Rahner, the Church's sacrament of confirmation is "the start of our conscious and willed witness to a faith that overcomes the world.... For confirmation is the sacrament of mission and of witness.... The Church expressly and unequivocally promises [the one confirmed] precisely a communication of the Spirit... who cannot be ousted from the world by the despairing no of the individual — the Spirit of the Father of Jesus, the Spirit of Jesus, a Spirit in whose efficacy and victory we trust."[37] The Church's sacrament of confirmation manifests fully the confirmation of everyday life.

Penance

Or take the person who in everyday life criticizes himself or herself, admits guilt, asks for forgiveness, is ready to confront the harsh truths about his or her existence, and attempts to eliminate individual and social evils — this person lives the metanoia, conversion, and penance of everyday life. Again, this penance of everyday life finds its fulfillment in the Church's sacrament of penance.

To Rahner, forgiveness is the most incomprehensible miracle of God's love because through it God communicates self to a person who had the audacity to say no to God. Furthermore, the word of God's forgiving love hidden in the depths of the human being has found its perfect expression and its historical irrevocability in the crucified and risen Lord. "This word of God's forgiveness," Rahner writes, "is Jesus Christ — the one in whom God's unconditional word of forgiveness has also become historically evident and irrevocable — and remains present in the community of those believing in this forgiveness in the Church. The Church is the fundamental sacrament of this word of God's forgiveness."[38] The truly penitent person, therefore, must not presuppose forgiveness but hear it spoken by the Church.

To one young man who claimed he had no need of the Church to love God, Rahner asked: "In your own life are you so obviously in an undisputed oneness and community with the holy God of eternal life that you do not even need Jesus' forgiving word through the Church's mediation for your guilt?"[39]

To another young man who claimed to prefer to confess his sins to God in the privacy of his room and who viewed sacramental confession as "meaningless," Rahner wrote that one can indeed confess in private. However, that does not make sacramental confession meaningless. "Have you never heard," Rahner wrote, "how many contemporary people are able to cope with their inner difficulties and troubles only when they try to clarify for themselves and to render surmountable their inner state of things by speaking about them to a psychologist or to a psychiatrist?"[40] Rahner isn't so certain that when this young man supposedly prays to God in private that a genuine, self-critical, transforming confession — which really corresponds to the seriousness of one's guilt before God — occurs as often as this young man may think. Rahner notes, too, how often a person's attitude really changes *during* the sacramental event.

Yet the sacramental words of absolution still cannot replace the person's willingness to strive for inner conversion.

Human beings, though, have an inner need to express their guilt and to hear words of forgiveness. Rahner finds it astonishing that people living in an age of talk shows would question the meaning of sacramental confession. "Sacramental confession," he writes, "is in its ultimate meaning an ever-renewed self-surrender of the total person to God's merciful grace, ... the courage to let our guilt be forgiven through the incomprehensible mystery we call God. Christianity is this message: we should allow ourselves to be forgiven. And the Church offers us the means: the sacrament of penance."[41]

Marriage

The sacrament of everyday life is also experienced by people who tacitly realize that love of neighbor is love of God, that in loving the other for his or her sake alone one falls lovingly into the Mystery that embraces all life. When two people dare to entrust their hearts, their lives, and their destinies to each other, thus abandoning self to the impenetrable mystery of another human being, this, to Rahner, is a miracle of love. When two people love each other, shed their egotism to surrender to each other, and remain faithful during difficult times, they experience the marriage of everyday life even prior to its fulfillment in sacramental marriage.[42]

"The pierced heart of the Redeemer," Rahner writes, "who upon the altar of the cross sacrificed Himself for His Bride, the Church, and allowed Himself to sink into death's infinite darkness, trusting that thus and by this means He would consign His spirit into His Father's hands"[43] is the source of the grace of marriage. The sacrament of marriage witnesses to this grace of Christ by making public and explicit one's commitment of love.

Ordination

Some people live with the hidden comprehension that they do not belong to themselves, that they are consecrated to the Mystery to whom they have said yes with all their being. They live in a way that awakens the experience of God in others. They awaken in others the question of eternal life. These people seem to dwell completely in God's explicit nearness and announce it, if only by their poise and bearing. They have the scent of the forgiving, loving God about them. They herald that love transcends all egotism, giving witness to the fact that we are most ourselves when we give ourselves away. These are the priests of everyday life even before the fullness of this consecration is bestowed through the Church's ordination.

To Rahner, a priest is one taken from men. After ordination he remains a man, that is, one who shares the lot of weak, sinful humanity. Priests are messengers who speak a human word filled with divine truth: "They say that God Himself is our life; they proclaim that death is not the end, that the world's cleverness is foolishness and shortsightedness.... And the man who is authorized to speak into the ever unique situation of the individual these words of the living God's sacramental presence and efficaciousness in the holy Church, that man we call the priest.... The priest is the man to whom the sacrifice of the Church, the liturgical repetition of Christ's Last Supper, is entrusted ... and ... this is after all the inmost and ultimate thing in priestly existence.... The priest is man, messenger of God's truth, dispenser of the divine mysteries, one who makes Christ's single sacrifice present again."[44]

The Anointing of the Sick

Persons who die every day by accepting — even if only anonymously — their radical finitude, that eternal life is born mysteriously from dying to self for others; those who affirm silently that they are not the source of their own existence; those who celebrate knowing that their own death can be the total handing over of themselves to God; those who comprehend that only Mystery is the final "cure" of human life — these people live the Anointing of the Sick even prior to its full sacramental reception.

Rahner points out that certain illnesses vividly remind us of our mortality and with that the fear of death which often secretly rules our lives. We know, of course, that we shall die. Still this knowledge usually remains abstract. On the other hand, illness often awakens us acutely and personally to the truth that we must die. "Illness is an experience," Rahner writes, "which brings us wholly face to face with ourselves, and therefore it is part of the history of our salvation."[45] Followers of Jesus believe that death can be a supreme test of faith, a test that can be passed only by faith in the grace of the One who knew how to die, Jesus Christ. Christians know also that not only is God with them when they die but also "the holy people of God are there in prayer around the loneliest sufferer. And if one of the holy community, even at the last moment and in silence, is present at the bedside of a sick person...then the eternal truth becomes manifest that we die in Christ, and are therefore always within His mysterious Body."[46]

Thus, the individual priest pronounces the word of faith for the healing of the sick person in the name of the whole Church and uses for this anointing the oil which the bishop consecrates on Holy Thursday, at the beginning of the yearly remembrance of our Lord's passion and death.

Summary

The divine-human drama, to Rahner, reaches its historical visibility in the crucified and risen Christ. He is the sacrament of God's self-offer. In his human reality God's victorious self-offer and its acceptance are irrevocably present and accessible. As the historical, social Body of Christ, the Church too is the sacrament of the world's salvation. What occurs in the sacraments of everyday life, to Rahner, "is seen by man in his dreary existence only through a haze, obscured by the banal ordinariness of life. It has to be reflected and elevated to the explicitness of the word and its sociological presence."[47] Thus, the Church's sacraments should be understood as the "epiphanization" or full flowering of the sacraments of everyday life. They explicitly symbolize and ritualize in the historical community of salvation what occurs always and everywhere in the world. In this way, Rahner distinguishes but refuses to separate the sacraments of everyday life from the Church's sacraments.

Notes

1. "Considerations of the Active Role of the Person in the Sacramental Event," *TI XIV*, 166–67.

2. Ibid., 167–68.

3. Ibid., 168.

4. *Visions and Prophecies*, 14, n. 12.

5. *Foundations of Christian Faith*, 322.

6. "The Church as the Subject of the Sending of the Spirit," *TI VII*, 188.

7. *Faith in a Wintry Season,* 155. My emphasis.

8. *Bekenntnisse,* 44.

9. *Faith in a Wintry Season,* 141–42.

10. "Ignatius of Loyola Speaks to a Modern Jesuit," *Ignatius of Loyola,* 27.

11. *Bekenntnisse,* 44.

12. *Faith in a Wintry Season,* 183.

13. Ibid., 177.

14. Ibid., 147–48.

15. Ibid., 111–12.

16. Ibid., 145.

17. *Foundations of Christian Faith,* 341. For an excellent summary of Rahner's view on the Church, see *Foundations of Christian Faith,* 322–401.

18. Ibid., 324.

19. Ibid., 401.

20. "The Church as the Subject of the Sending of the Spirit," *TI VII,* 189–90.

21. "The Foundation of Belief," *TI XVI,* 21.

22. "Dogmatic Notes on 'Ecclesiological Piety,'" *TI V,* 365.

23. *Foundations of Christian Faith,* 357–58.

24. *Faith in a Wintry Season,* 80.

25. "The Church of Sinners," *TI VI,* 260–61.

26. Ibid., 262–63.

27. *Meditations on the Sacraments,* trans. Salvator Attanasio, James M. Quigley, S.J., and Dorothy White (New York: Seabury, 1977), xv.

28. *Faith in a Wintry Season,* 40.

29. "The Presence of the Lord in the Christian Community at Worship," *TI X,* 83.

30. For an alternate translation, see "Considerations of the Active Role of the Person in the Sacramental Event," *TI XIV,* 169.

31. "On the Theology of Worship," *TI XIX,* 161–84. Also see "The Eucharist in Our Daily Lives," *TI VII,* 211–26; *Meditations on the Sacraments,* 29–41.

32. "Theological Reflections on the Priestly Image of Today and Tomorrow," *TI XII,,* 44.

33. "Considerations of the Active Role of the Person in the Sacramental Event," *TI XIV,* 169–70.

34. *Karl Rahner in Dialogue,* 60.

35. "Considerations of the Active Role of the Person in the Sacramental Event," *TI XIV,* 172.

36. *Meditations on the Sacraments,* 2–4.

37. Ibid., 18–26.

38. Ibid., 52.
39. *Is Christian Life Possible Today?* 48–49. Translation emended.
40. Ibid., 95. Translated emended.
41. *Meditations on the Sacraments,* 52–59.
42. *Karl Rahner in Dialogue,* 122.
43. *Meditations on the Sacraments,* 77.
44. Ibid., 63–67.
45. Ibid., 80.
46. Ibid., 82–83.
47. "On the Theology of Worship," *TI XIX,* 146.

Chapter 8

Karl Rahner — Teacher of Christian Life

When asked by an interviewer to sum up what being a Christian means for him, Rahner said: "To be a Christian means to adore God, to love him, to entrust oneself obediently to his incomprehensibility and to his incomprehensible dominion. It means to know that after death there is life eternal in the direct vision of God. Jesus Christ supports and legitimates this total relationship to God. Because of Christ, his cross, his resurrection, and the unsurpassable unity between God and man given in him we can trust that our life's task of entering into direct relationship with God will really succeed through God's victorious grace. That people who because of Jesus Christ thus dare to entrust themselves to God form a community of faith which is called Church, that this community of faith has a history, a social structure, a structure that binds the individual — along with everything else that even the ordinary Christian knows about the Church — then all this is really obvious. It is also self-evident that Christians and their Church — empowered by the Holy Spirit — must stand up and work for justice, love and freedom in a world loved as God's creation."[1]

In another context Rahner makes the seemingly banal assertion that a "Christian is simply man as he is, . . . a creature who in darkness is oriented towards light, and who is life in the midst of death."[2] A genuine Christian accepts unreservedly the entirety of concrete human life. He or she musters the courage to accept unconditionally human existence and utters no final protest against it. Of course a Christian is baptized, participates in the Church's liturgical life, and lives according to the norms of Christian morality. Still what ultimately characterizes a Christian is "that he accepts himself just as he is, and does this without making anything an idol, without leaving anything out, and without closing himself to the totality of what in the ultimate depths of reality is inescapably imposed upon man as his task."[3]

Christian Freedom

Rahner emphasizes Christian life as a life of freedom, an openness to everything without exception. To be sure, to be open to God's incomprehensible truth and love requires a person to be closed to sin and to fight against evil with all one's might. Rahner is not naive. He knows that we are not pure freedom, that many factors outside the range of freedom determine every person's life, and that many internal and external factors situate our freedom. "But a Christian believes," Rahner writes, "that there is a path to freedom which lies in going through this imprisonment. We do not seize it by force, but rather it is given to us by God insofar as he gives himself to us throughout all the imprisonments of our existence."[4]

During a Mass for students who had fashioned an altar by using a plank supported by two motorcycles, Rahner gave what may have been his last informal homily. He told students to stop blaming their parents, society, the government, and the Church for their lot and to remember the incredible depths of their own freedom: they had the capacity to say yes or no with their entire being to the God of love. He also encouraged them to hope as Christians, to look beyond themselves "to the promise of the living God that He will triumph over the risks of human existence with his powerful love."[5]

Christian Realism

This hope is not naive but is grounded in a radical pessimistic realism which rejects any and all ideologies, even those which parade under the name "Christian." That Rahner rejects any quick fixes to the human situation may be one of the significant bequests from his spiritual legacy. "The real and total and comprehensive task of a Christian as a Christian," Rahner says, "is to be a human being, a human being, of course, whose depths are divine."[6] Because our ultimate depths open out onto God, Christian life must be an acceptance of human existence. This fundamental openness to God allows a Christian to view human existence the way it is — "dark and bitter and hard, and as an unfathomable and radical risk."[7]

Christian realism understands and accepts that everything dies, that even the most precious and beautiful things of life must pass through death. "Christianity," to Rahner, "is the religion which recognizes a man who was nailed to a cross and on it died a violent death as a sign of victory and as a realistic expression of human life, and it has made this its own sign.... Why? Evidently it is supposed to remind us that we may not be dishonest and try to suppress the hardness and darkness and death in our existence, and that as Christians we evidently do not have a right not to want to have anything to do with this aspect of life until we have no choice. At that point death comes to us, but we have not gone to death. But death is the only passage to the life which really does not die any more and which does not experience death at its inner core."[8]

Christians have been baptized into Christ's death. They drink from the chalice of the death of Christ at Eucharist. Rahner says that "only when we live out this pessimistic realism and renounce every ideology which makes absolute a particular sector of human existence and makes it an idol, it is only then that it is possible for us to allow God to give us the hope which really makes us free."[9]

The hope that makes us free flows from the Christian experience that God and God alone is our absolute future. The Christian will not so desperately cling to anything worldly that only death itself can wrench it away. Neither will the Christian take the darkness of this world so seriously that he or she can no longer enjoy the glimmers of eternal light beyond it that punctuate human life. The Christian is therefore one who makes absolute neither this life nor death.

The Pluralism of Human Life

Christians must also accept what Rahner calls the pluralism of human existence. The human person is a biological, psychological, physical, social, spiritual reality who must not only love God but also live and work in a pluralistic world. No one can integrate all these plural dimensions of human existence to master and control them. "If a Christian," Rahner says, "really professes that God can be and is God so very much that he can establish in reality something which is really different from himself in its absolute and incalculable plurality, then a Christian can and must open himself in real trust and without reservations to this pluralism in human existence."[10]

The mysticism of everyday life thus takes place precisely in a variegated daily life. The primordial experience of God that haunts every human heart is mediated only by a real, genuine self-abandonment to the plurality of human existence. "And through and in everything," Rahner states, "[the Christian] can find in trust the very God who willed this incalculable pluralism in the world. He willed this so that precisely by going through this pluralism man would have an intimation that all of this is encompassed by the eternal mystery."[11]

Christian Sinfulness

Moral struggle also characterizes Christian existence. Christians always experience the difference between what they are and what they should be, a difference they must accept. "A correct acceptance," Rahner says, "indeed always includes an attempt to overcome this difference in an upward direction, and hence it includes a 'no' to something and a 'yes' to something else and better. For this difference is always found as something concrete, not as something abstract."[12]

Paradoxically, the Christian "experiences the struggle of moral striving as an inescapable datum of his own experience. ... He is always one who fails, one who always falls short of his task.... Hence he is always a person who recognizes that he is encompassed by God's love, and at the same time he is a sinner in some sense and to some incalculable degree.... As a Christian, then, he is always ... both justified and a sinner at the same time."[13]

According to Rahner, one sins by making absolute or idolizing anything finite. In practice this involves closing oneself to God's self-communication. Sin is an unwillingness to be utterly open to God from the most interior part of one's being. The sinner is ultimately "a person who does not believe that the infinite fullness of all values dwells in unity beyond this immediately tangible reality, and that this fullness offers himself to him in his self-communication through grace as the fullness and as the ultimate meaning of his existence."[14] One also sins by freely misusing or disdaining what God has created, the very things which mediate our experience of God.

The Christian in Society

Rahner points out that Christians now live in "diaspora," that is, in societies in which they are often a minority. Less and less does society support Christian life. Thus genuine Christian faith must be more a matter of free decision, personal responsibility, and a personal avowal of faith and less a matter of having been born in a Christian society and family. Authentic Christian life, Rahner writes, must emerge "from the innermost center of our own existence and not merely as a fulfillment of religious conventions prevailing in Christianity and in the Church. Spirituality — Christian spirituality — is the active participation in the death of Jesus and, since he is risen, in that death as successful and as assumed into that ineffable, incomprehensible, uncontrollable, unmanipulatable ultimate mystery which every person, as Aquinas would say, calls God."[15]

Because the Christian is spirit-in-world, he or she must accept the world without idolizing or condemning it. The mature Christian has the courage to make responsible decisions for action in the world, for making life more worth living. In fact the mature Christian should practice the genuine virtues of the world and allow himself or herself to be educated in courage, joy, duty, perseverance, hard work, and love.

Rahner renounces any ghetto-like Christian living that clings in a reactionary way to the past and that in a comfortable cowardice renounces all claims to influence the course of political life. Christianity demands a political form of living which presupposes a right to cooperate in public life. The Christian need not seek special favors from the state, but neither should he or she permit Christian values to be eliminated from public life. "We are quite ready," Rahner writes, "to enter into discussion, are anxious for a fair and open dialogue with all, and are even ready to entertain reasonable compromise. On the other hand we refuse to be intimidated when we are stigmatized as bigots, narrow-minded reactionaries, or intolerant, merely because we are of the opinion that Christian ideas too must be allowed to exert their due influence in the sphere of political life. We have only to compare our position with that of the false liberalism which maintains that political life can and must undergo an ideological process of sterilization, and that creeds and conscience should only be allowed a voice in the churches or the clubs of humanistic society."[16]

Salvation, to Rahner, concerns the entire person in every dimension of his or her life. Genuine love of neighbor may often demand that a Christian take a political stand. Rahner sees an intrinsic unity between religion, morality, and justice.

Christian Evangelization

The mature Christian will also take his or her missionary responsibility seriously. Christians must do more than strengthen their own faith. They must do more than simply dialogue and collaborate with unbelievers in the secular sphere. They must also take seriously their obligation to help others become Christian.

On the other hand, "Christians have to get used to the fact," Rahner says, "that their belonging to the Church, their baptism, creedal confession and cult is not finally the affirmation of something in contradiction to unbelievers but is rather a bringing to historical and social visibility of the inner reality of their being. This is certainly offered to their freedom and may well have already been freely accepted. What we are talking about is the yes of God to unbelievers and their possible but secret yes to God."[17]

Genuine Christianity is the full flowering of God's grace already at work in unbelievers in the seriousness and responsibility of their moral life and in their efforts to deal with the ultimate and unavoidable questions of existence. Seeing "unbelievers" as anonymous Christians will prevent mature Christians from fanatical proselytizing, from rejecting anyone with a different worldview, and from a skeptical relativism which is in fact a tacit betrayal of Christianity's claim to be the absolute religion and the best interpretation of the meaning of human life. Mature Christians also know that "Christians are not just Christians and non-Christians are by no means just non-Christians."[18] In other words, Christians too are sinners, and non-Christians too live by the grace of Christ.

However, not just any Christian is entrusted a missionary task. "The task of evangelizing unbelievers," Rahner writes, "can only be undertaken by those lay persons who themselves have an authentic Church experience, who are part of a living eucharistic community in which people have accepted Christianity by a personal decision. They must themselves have appropriated it in a personal and original way and not just (more or less) be carrying it on as a tradition and as a part of their social conditioning."[19] Mature Christians should also focus more on the essence of Christianity — the orientation of human beings to the absolute and yet self-communicating mystery of God mediated historically in Jesus Christ.

The witness of their Christian lives is perhaps the most important requirement for the missionary dimension of their work in secular society. "Their practice, their constantly renewed hope, their objectivity and selflessness, their unconditional and unrewarded fidelity to conscience, and so on," Rahner says, "can provoke unbelievers to wonder about the ultimate motives and attitudes out of which the actions of Christians flow. Thus, their secular life itself becomes a witness for Christ and for his grace."[20]

Christ's injunction to "go therefore and make disciples of all nations, baptizing them in the name of the Father and of the Son and of the Holy Spirit" (Matt. 28:19) is not the sole reason for Christian missionary activity in a secular society. Genuine human life depends upon social interaction and dialogue in and through which people share themselves with one another. Unity with God and Christ is the basis and fulfillment of all other human ways of being united. As Rahner says, "since Christian love of neighbor, which is rooted in grace, seeks to unite people at the deepest level of their existence, it cannot in principle refuse the neighbor help in achieving salvation, the fulfillment of human existence. A fundamental denial of a genuine missionary obligation of the laity would be a clerical misunderstanding of the Church."[21]

The Mature Attitude and Church Teachings

Rahner himself embodies many of the ideals of the mature Christian. For example, when asked about the partial censorship imposed on him shortly before the Second Vatican Council, he replied: "If a theologian doesn't merely parrot the obvious, but tries to think out this or that on his own accord and at his own risk, he cannot expect a priori that everything is going to proceed without causing any difficulties for his colleagues and for the Church. I hope this doesn't sound like an old man's euphoric, serene reminiscences, but in looking back on this negative experience I just don't feel that it was all that dramatic."[22] Rahner knew that Aquinas, Suarez, and other theologians had problems with Church officials, and thus he could say: "But you see from this that in the old days a Catholic theologian didn't get as worked up about this sort of thing as one does today."[23] On the other hand, neither does Rahner necessarily approve of certain "Roman methods."

Rahner maintains that there must be public opinion and criticism in the Church. "We can disagree over 'how' to do that. I think, however, that even if one disagrees about this or that concrete aspect, still a Catholic has the obligation to retain certain forms of respect toward the pope and the bishops."[24] However, obeying legitimate authority doesn't mean that one must applaud it.

When an interviewer raised the burning issue of people leaving the Church, Rahner replied: "I would like to say that this phenomenon of quietly leaving the Church should be a much greater incentive for the Church, the bishops, the religion teachers, priests, and theologians to present the Christian message and the Christian way of life in newer and more attractive ways. [Nonetheless] we shouldn't always blame God and his 'representatives' for the large number of people leaving."[25]

Rahner admits that the Gospel is often preached in a boring way. However, he notes that many contemporary sociological factors — which have nothing to do with the Church — also greatly influence people. "There are even families," he says, "in which the parents are marvelous human beings who properly raise their children and yet experience terrible setbacks in raising them. So a good number of people leaving the Church is practically quite unavoidable."[26]

Rahner eschews making one's subjectivity the norm for all things. "We should admit," he says, "that there are things in life which don't speak to us at the present time but to which, with more experience and greater maturity, we might someday have access. For this reason I would advise a young woman who might turn up her nose at any mention of the virginity of Mary, 'Just wait a bit. Let's talk later about all this. It is neither a disgrace nor a sin if you are unable now to understand this teaching of the Church. You should not, however, absolutize your present position, but rather see it as only a moment in your far from complete personal history.' "[27] This advice, of course, pertains to other Church teachings.

Rahner is especially impatient with Christians who deny outright any of the Church's defined and irreformable teachings. The mature Christian doesn't say, for example, that he or she is utterly and completely certain that the pope is not infallible. "In my opinion," Rahner states, "Küng here clearly contradicts teaching that is obligatory for a Catholic. And I have often said this directly to him.... [He] is wrong when he affirms that the Church can err even in those cases where in its own understanding it makes a judgment in a definite and irreformable way."[28] And yet Rahner wrote to Rome on Küng's behalf. He may have disagreed with Küng theologically, but neither did he approve of all Roman methods.

Although Rahner never denies any Church dogmas, he does not hesitate to say that some are more important than others. For example, the doctrine of papal infallibility to him is not as important for Christian life as the dogmas about Jesus' salvific death and resurrection. "Dogmas have very differing degrees of importance. Of course my faith in Jesus Christ means much more to me than the teaching of the First Vatican Council about the pope. The first is very important to me; the other is secondary, which is not to say it does not bind."[29]

On the other hand, there are many teachings of the Church's magisterium which do not enjoy the certainty of a final and defining ex cathedra decision. "There are teachings in regard to which the Church can err; there are ... declarations which are reformable."[30] This certainly does not mean that a mature

Christian can ignore or consider them irrelevant for Christian life. For example, a person would be acting imprudently and rashly who rejected the best medical opinion concerning a certain medical procedure, even though the experts were not infallible and at a later date were found to be in error.

Rahner also says that the Church is not a debating club. Decision in many cases must be made, even when the Church's teaching authority cannot do so in an infallible way. However, cases of reformable decisions leave room for discussion and even for a further decision of the individual's mature and responsible conscience. Rahner says this expressly about the Church's ban on the use of artificial contraceptives.

His attitude toward the ordination of women is instructive. "First of all," he says, "we must hold on to the fact that the Congregation of the Faith has declared in an authentic but non-defined way that according to the will of Christ women may not be ordained in the Church. I have openly presented my own opposing views. That is, I am not bound to declare the teaching of the Congregation of the Faith, for which I have great formal respect, as absolutely binding and obligatory for me. We must leave open the question of who really is right.

"Furthermore, it seems to me that many Christians today suffer from a remarkable schizophrenia. On the one hand, in a sort of demeaning theology, they seem to perceive the priest more or less as a ritualist, as a secondary functionary of a societally constituted Church. On the other hand, these same Christians get all upset if such an office is not allowed to them or to certain groups. Personally I can easily imagine that one day, through a further development in society's thinking, the Catholic Church will acknowledge the ordination of women with eucharistic powers to preside over communities."[31] And I suspect that Rahner would hold this same position, even in light of recent Church statements that its teaching against the ordination of women is "definitive," given the disagreement among theologians as to whether "definitive" means infallible.

However, Rahner genuinely respects even non-infallible Church teachings. When pressed by an interviewer on the issue of women's ordination, Rahner asked: "Do you have, on the basis of a personal inclination, the right to demand an official function in the Church?"[32] When the woman interviewer said that she could always change Churches, Rahner replied: "If you are convinced that the Catholic Church is simply one of many conditioned and arbitrary religious groupings, all having the same worth and validity, then naturally you can convert to a Protestant church in order to become a pastor. A serious Catholic would have to say: 'I would like very much to be ordained; not only that, but I am convinced that in two or three hundred years there will be no laws against it in the Catholic Church. For now, however, I simply have to accept this restriction on my life.' Who doesn't experience curtailments, limitations, and disappointments in regard to subjective and totally legitimate life plans?"[33]

If one finds this pastoral advice too facile, one should remember that Rahner's disagreement with Church authority over the ban on artificial contraception cost him the cardinalate. Rahner said, too, that it was immature to believe that taking a stand against those with authority might not sometimes be costly.

When his friend Johann Baptist Metz urged him to "be far more radical, upset, and angry about many things in the Church,"[34] Rahner replied: "We who have been baptized and endowed with light and grace by the Holy Spirit, we who have our final hope in eternal life with God, we must be much more sensitive to the scandals, the pitiful behavior, and the petty-bourgeois mentality in our Church. But even here we should exercise a little calmness and patience. After all, we are all sinners."[35] Thus, Rahner is not only self-critical, but also critical "even of the criticism that is often legitimately brought out against the institutional Church."[36] He did not fear criticizing the critics of the official Church. In the final analysis, Rahner says: "I have no difficulty in accepting the existing institutional Church as the concrete form of the charismatic Church."[37]

The Gospels clearly teach, to Rahner, that renouncing marriage for the sake of the Kingdom is God's gift, a charismatic calling. If celibacy for the sake of Christ were to die out in the Church, the Church would no longer be the Church of Jesus Christ. A voluntary renunciation does not disdain marriage, but considers it a great good that may be given up for Christ's sake. However, that there be a celibate clergy is *a* principle but not *the* principle in the Catholic Church. Pointing to the Eastern Catholics in union with Rome who have a married clergy, Rahner asks why there shouldn't be a married clergy in the West.

On the other hand, he finds some of the emphasis on a married clergy the result of a petty-bourgeois mentality too much connected with today's overemphasis on self-fulfillment and sexual pleasure. Rahner wonders too why so many non-Catholics take so much interest in the Church's position on a celibate clergy when it really should not concern them.

To an interviewer who regarded the Church's sexual morality as especially difficult for young people, Rahner replied that he wished young people would understand "that sexuality is an area of their freedom, and indeed of their responsible freedom, of their moral duty, and of their destiny. Without a doubt you cannot bracket sexuality out of the area of moral responsibility. That in no way means that sexuality is nothing more than an exercise field for morality and moral self-control. Why shouldn't young persons experience their sexuality in a positive way? It is just that sexuality must be viewed as a partial task which is ultimately drawn into the totality of a human being's life task. This task is essentially a moral one that must answer to God."[38]

Rahner concedes that the Church's past sexual norms may not have been correct in every instance. Some of her traditional attitudes may have been unfair to a genuinely human and thus Christian sexuality. Premarital intercourse, he says, might in some circumstances be Christian.

On the other hand, Rahner brings up short a young man who had sexual relations with a few women and then with his wife for a few years before marriage but who never felt guilty.[39] He questions whether the young man's relationships with these women were really as deep as he claims or whether he was not casual and dismissive. Was the premarital relationship with his wife really so harmless? This period of lack of total commitment could have turned out otherwise. Does his present experience of marriage call into question some of his past behavior? Is he really as self-critical and honest with himself as he claims? In short, was and is this person truly a mature Christian?

Of course history conditions Christian morality and therefore sexual morality. "To be sure," Rahner says, "historicity does not mean that one can expect that the Church will proclaim in a future sexual morality precisely the opposite of what it teaches today. Love, sexuality, the binding together of two human beings in a total relationship, fidelity, self-control, among other things as well, obviously will always remain valid. For this reason the Church must proclaim such values even these days. Doesn't a laxness which is fundamentally inhuman rule today precisely in these things? And it is far from proven that everything which the Church has to say in the area of human morality is 'old-fashioned,' and that it merely belongs to the past history of moral norms. It is thoroughly possible that even very hard demands can be basically freeing for human beings."[40]

Rahner respects the hierarchical Church because Christ is its Head. He accepts legitimate authority, "office," in the Church as part of its essence. The Church of Jesus Christ, however, is animated by the Holy Spirit and includes the entire people of God, their charisms, and their faith-instinct. Clearly no single authority in the Church holds all the power.

Rahner writes movingly and convincingly for a declericalized, decentralized, open, ecumenical, servant Church of real spirituality.[41] He predicts, too, that the future Church will be more democratic, but not a carbon copy of the democracy that should exist in a secular society. "Democracy in the Church," Rahner writes, "means simply, in the first place, that lay people should have as active and responsible a part in its life and decisions as possible. It means more precisely that their active participation should be institutionalized in canon law."[42]

On the other hand, Rahner does not share the overly romantic view about democracy in the Church. "How can you concretely conceive of democratization in a Church that has several billion members," he asks. "There are a thousand questions. Who is to be elected from the base? Would you include those who haven't attended church for thirty years and who bear a grudge against the pope? Should such persons be elected? Why couldn't democratization of shared decision-making be initiated at lower levels?"[43]

Rahner has great sympathy for political and liberation theologies and even for Marxist-tinged groups which use these theologies to criticize unjust social structures to achieve a more humane world. These theologies and groups rightly reject the overly individualistic spiritualities of the past and stress the public, social nature of the Gospel. Rahner disagrees with bishops and others who demonize these theologies and groups or who deem Marxism "unacceptable."[44] He asks that the Church be patient with these experiments. And because of his Christian convictions and his desire to be found worthy on Judgment Day, Rahner says that if he lived in South America, he would indeed be a leftist in opposition to the capitalism existing there.[45]

On the other hand, neither does he find everything good in leftist Christian movements nor does he find it necessary to break with his social milieu and head off for Cuba.[46] "Where can I find Marxist governments under which one can still call Christianity free," he asks.[47] When he met the controversial priest Ernesto Cardenal, then Minister of Culture in the Nicaraguan government, Rahner said: "With all modesty, although he embraced me warmly, I found what he said from both political and theological points of view to be a fair amount of nonsense. He affirmed that with the Sandinistas in Nicaragua the kingdom of God had finally broken in. We heard ideological fantasy such as that there were no more prisons and that everyone loved one another. In terms of such experiences I would say that if a bishop or pope is a little more careful in regard to some developments in the Third World than some of their critics, it is by no means a priori certain that their position is unreasonable."[48]

Rahner also had a jaundiced eye with respect to the tendency of these theologies and groups to reduce the Christian message to this world and to use God for political ends. What could they say to someone dying of cancer? Furthermore, he states, "I did once say in regard to certain theologians of political and liberation theology: All well and good, but my mother was an authentic Christian and she never took a political stand in her life."[49]

Conclusion

Let us conclude this chapter with a brief selection from one of Rahner's homilies for Pentecost, entitled "Fear of the Spirit."

This selection illustrates indirectly his own view of the mature Christian as one who holds a middle ground and discerns the spirits. "Even in the life of the Church as such," he says, "this fear of the Holy Spirit can be found. Fear can be perceived among the 'traditionalists.' They fear risks and experiments the results of which are not known in advance. They don't want to hear any formulations of faith with which they have not been familiar from childhood onwards, as if a proposition and the Spirit which it attests were simply identical. They want to have unity in the variety of the Church in such a way that they can thoroughly understand this unity and take it under their own control. The tradition which they defend — as such rightly — is for them the land of the fathers, now definitely acquired and only needing to be inhabited and governed, not a station on a pilgrimage, beckoning them on further, even though of course in the direction in which they had hitherto been moving. And if they admit and profess in theory the doctrine of divine unrest in the Church, known as the Holy Spirit, it is only in order really to have the right to refuse the demands of this incalculable Spirit in practical life.

"On the other hand, we get the impression that those also are often afraid of the Holy Spirit who proudly call themselves or are suspected by others of being 'progressives.' For real confidence in the power of the Holy Spirit in his Church implies also the hopeful faith that he constantly prevails in this Church with his power of renewal. But why then are these 'progressives' so often irritated and impatient? How is the faith in God's Spirit constantly renewing 'the face of the earth' of the Church compatible with the peevish threat to leave the Church if she does not soon undergo a thorough change, while granting her somewhat optimistically a brief period in which to become again a home which they don't have to leave?

"Don't the 'progressives' also dictate to the Holy Spirit where he has to be active? Namely, at a critical distance from the Church which is identified with office and tradition, in purely social commitment, in the will for the unity of Christians at all costs. Not, however, in worship of God, in love for a real fresh and blood neighbor, in fraternal patience and magnanimous understanding for those of his brethren who have to serve the Church in an office to which they never quite do justice (how could it be otherwise?), with good will and an open mind even toward initiatives which emerge from official sources in the Church, in an open-mindedness without which, whether we admit it or not, we remain complacently and autocratically entangled in our own subjectivity. Are the 'progressives' not often afraid of the Holy Spirit when they fear death, which means here fear of the mute, unrewarded sacrifice in the service of the Church and of her mission, a sacrifice which cannot be justified in terms of a will for a merely intramundane future?

"If the question is put to 'traditionalists' and 'progressives' in this way, as to whether they are not both afraid of the Spirit, the double question must not be suspected as a cheap, dialectical reconciliation of the two standpoints, nor be misused by professors and, today, by bishops who are inclined to advise a cheap 'both this and that' or a 'golden mean.' Of course there are appropriate middle ways, and certainly the extremes of the *terribles simplificateurs* are stupid and can lead only to disaster. Certainly among the Christian virtues are moderation, patience, and the realism which is not fanatical and does not want to turn the world too quickly into a paradise soon to become a concentration camp of universal forced happiness.

"But the Holy Spirit is simply not a compromise between intramundane antagonisms, not the golden mean, not the holiness of narrow-minded mediocrity. The Holy Spirit in particular must not be understood as one side of the dialectic, the other being made up of the letter, the law, the institution, and rational calculation. Rather is the Spirit the one who constantly blasts open all such empirical, dialectical unities of opposites (although these have their justification) and sweeps them into the movement directed toward the incomprehensible God, who is not merely another particular factor in the world and in the counterplay and interplay of forces."[50]

Notes

1. *Karl Rahner in Dialogue,* 329–30. Translation emended. In "Intellectual Honesty and Christian Faith," *TI VII,* 60, Rahner gives another summary of what Christianity is: "Christianity is the explicit and socially (ecclesiastically) constituted affirmation that the absolute

mystery who inevitably holds sway in and over our existence, who is called God — that this forgiving and divinizing mystery communicates himself to us in our history as free subjects and that in Jesus Christ this self-communication manifests itself in history as victorious and irreversible." Translation emended.

2. *Foundations of Christian Faith*, 402 and 407.

3. Ibid., 402.

4. Ibid., 403.

5. Ibid.

6. Ibid.

7. Ibid.

8. Ibid., 404.

9. Ibid.

10. Ibid., 406.

11. Ibid., 406–7.

12. Ibid., 408.

13. Ibid., 410–11.

14. Ibid., 409.

15. "The Spirituality of the Priest in the Light of His Office," *TI XIX*, 122.

16. "The Christian in His World," *TI VII*, 91.

17. "The Missionary Task of Christians," *The Content of Faith*, 593.

18. Karl Rahner and Karl-Heinz Weger, *Our Christian Faith: Answers for the Future*, trans. Francis McDonagh (New York: Crossroad Publishing Co., 1981), 118. Henceforth referred to as *Our Christian Faith*.

19. "The Missionary Task of Christians," *The Content of Faith*, 594.

20. Ibid., 595.

21. Ibid.

22. *Faith in a Wintry Season*, 15. Translation emended.

23. *Karl Rahner — I Remember*, 63.

24. *Faith in a Wintry Season*, 12.

25. Ibid., 175.

26. Ibid.

27. Ibid., 90.

28. Ibid., 151.

29. Ibid., 95.

30. Ibid., 143.

31. Ibid., 101.

32. Ibid., 153.

33. Ibid.

34. Ibid., 146.

35. Ibid.

36. Ibid.

37. Ibid., 147.

38. Ibid., 112.

39. *Is Christian Life Possible Today?* 98–102.

40. *Faith in a Wintry Season,* 113.

41. See *The Shape of the Church to Come,* trans. Edward Quinn (New York: Seabury Press, 1974); "Dream of the Church," *TI XX,* trans. Edward Quinn (New York: Crossroad Publishing Co., 1981), 133–42; "The Perennial Actuality of the Papacy," *TI XXII,* 191–207. The latter two essays are especially compelling Rahnerian visions of the future Church.

42. *The Content of Faith,* 491.

43. *Faith in a Wintry Season,* 72.

44. Ibid., 62.

45. *Karl Rahner in Dialogue,* 274.

46. *Faith in a Wintry Season,* 61–62.

47. Ibid., 63.

48. Ibid., 146.

49. *Karl Rahner in Dialogue,* 273.

50. *The Great Church Year,* 217–18.

Chapter 9

Karl Rahner — Teacher of the Last Things

The contemporary lack of Christian preaching on the way our history of freedom becomes final, on eternal life, and on God's judgment bothers Rahner. Thus, one of the most striking gifts from his spiritual legacy is his teaching on the so-called "Last Things." No contemporary theologian or even Church Father has written so cogently on the Christian meaning of old age. Moreover, few contemporary theologians have so profoundly recast Christian thinking about death, purgatory, bodily resurrection, hell, and heaven.

Old Age

Rahner speaks of the challenge of growing old.[1] In former times old people were revered and rewarded with positions of honor. Now the elderly tend to be pushed aside and referred to as a costly burden on society. However, by sheer force of numbers, skill, and financial independence, the elderly can often exert considerable, but sometimes resented, political power.

When asked by an interviewer how he experienced his old age, Rahner said: "Well, especially in our day there are many people who speak glowingly about old age with often heart-rending speeches. To be sure, a peaceful, ripe, wise old age — perhaps filled with reminiscences — exists. Yet, to put it quite soberly, there is also the kind of old age that comes closer and closer to death — an exhausting old age, an old age redolent in a variety of ways in which one feels pushed quickly along the rails of death and painfully sees life coming to an end. I believe that a Christian must also cope soberly and without illusions with this sort of old age too because he or she does have a 'hope against all hope,' as St. Paul would say."[2]

Rahner bluntly said that one should live as best as one can when one is elderly. If one likes to walk, to spend time with friends, to take up a hobby, all well and good.[3] When these things no longer work, however, that is all right too. One should nonetheless strive to maintain one's hope in eternal life.

When pressed by an interviewer about how he would cope with the diminished energy that usually accompanies old age, Rahner said: "They say of Saint Albert the Great that toward the end of his life he forgot all his great theology... [and] could only pray the 'Hail Mary.' Well, if that happens to someone, then that person too must manage. If one is really on one's deathbed, then indeed everything ceases — perhaps even the ability to react to such a situation. If even this is taken away, all the better. Then, I believe, one finds oneself even more in God's hands. And one is safer and more secure there in God's hands than where one supposes one must be in total control of one's own self."[4]

Rahner views old age as "a grace — both mission and risk — not given to everyone, just as there are other possibilities and situations which must be undergone in a Christian way and appraised as graces which are granted to some and withheld from others. That must be seen and accepted as part of 'God's will.' In this connection we should not take facile comfort in the ultimately erroneous thought that old age, like many other life situations, is a merely external situation which does not terminate in the definitive sequel of life but is merely like a costume in which a person plays a role in the theater of life which remains extraneous to himself, which he then simply removes at death, which does not — even transformed — end in the personal finality we call eternal life. Such an opinion (only superficially pious) does not take the human person's history really seriously. 'Eternity' is the transformed definitiveness of history itself. Whether a person dies young or dies old, he takes this temporal destiny of his into his definitiveness as an inner moment of it.

"Growing old is therefore a really serious matter. It is a grace, a mission, and contains the risk of radical failure. Growing old is a stage of human and Christian life which (like every other stage of life) is irreplaceably important and broaches no substitutes. This is particularly true since old age must be understood not simply as life's running out but as life's 'coming to definitiveness,' even when that happens under the paralyzing influence of slow biological death. The same thing may be said of old age — more or less — as is said in a Christian interpretation of death. We must always understand that we undergo death — not in medical expiration — but in the length and breadth of our entire life. We undergo death in ways indeed befitting each individual stage."[5]

Rahner takes all phases of life seriously because: (1) the human person is historical by nature; (2) the human person becomes through his free decisions throughout his history what he shall be for all eternity. And the person graced with old age must take into account that *now* is an especially good time to sum himself up the way he wants to be eternally.

Death

During a private audience with Pope John Paul II a few years before Rahner's death, the pope asked him how things were going. Rahner said candidly: "I am retired, living in Munich, and waiting to die."[6] A year later when asked by an interviewer why he left Munich for Innsbruck, Rahner replied that he was going there to die and wanted to be with people who would pray for him during that time. Rahner's last words to me were: "I must die."

On numerous occasions interviewers asked Rahner if he feared death. "I think that fear of death," he said, "belongs to the nature of death, and I am not of the opinion that a Christian must necessarily die as a Stoic or as a Socrates. If a Christian can do so, there is no objection against it. But he or she need not. A Christian can also imitate Jesus in the Garden of Olives or pray as he did on the cross, 'My God, my God, why have you forsaken me?' and then add, 'Into your hands I commend my spirit, into your hands, O absolutely incomprehensible God.' That too is possible. In other words I can confidently meet death and also accept the fear of death in a final confidence and surrender."[7]

Despite his healthy, natural fear of death, the faith-filled Rahner denies that death is simply the end.[8] In fact, death is really handing one's total self over to God, just as the crucified Jesus did. "No one escapes having to die with Jesus Christ," Rahner says. "The whole Christian life consists in weaving together realities for whose structuring one can offer no formula that is really practical. When you are young, perhaps you think that you have a grand, maybe even an ideal, theory into which everything fits. But in time, to a certain extent, such an ideological view of life vanishes. And nothing remains for you but to hand over to the eternal God your actions, your disappointments, your sins, your successes — your whole life. Only God can make sense out of this mess.... To everyone I can say: 'The one incomprehensible mystery of God is a reality and you must die into it. At the same time you have in Jesus... the promise that this leap into God's incomprehensibility has really succeeded.'... Death would have to be interpreted negatively if we did *not* die with Jesus, the crucified and risen One."[9]

One of Rahner's most beautiful prayers focuses on death. "Then You [God] will be the final Word," Rahner prays, "the only one that remains, the one we shall never forget. Then at last, everything will be quiet in death; then I shall have finished with all my learning and suffering. Then will begin the great silence in which no other sound will be heard but You, O Word resounding from eternity to eternity. Then all human words will have grown dumb. Being and knowing, understanding and experience will have become one and the same. 'I shall know as I am known'; I shall understand what You have been saying to me all along, namely You Yourself. No more human words, no more concepts, no more pictures will stand between us. You Yourself will be the one exultant word of love and life filling out every corner of my soul.... You Yourself are my knowledge, experience, and love. You are the God of the one and only knowledge that is eternal, the knowledge that is bliss without end."[10]

Rahner does not share the view of some theologians that the moment of *medical* death brings with it a special light or grace which allows one to turn one's entire life upside down. He states the seemingly obvious truth that "death may occur very uneventfully and unconsciously."[11] Of course, the time of theological death and medical expiration may more or less coincide.

On the other hand, Rahner says that "somewhere within our lives there happens — or there may at least happen — an absolute letting go, an absolute yielding of everything. This may constitute death in the *theological* sense, which may ultimately consist in the unconditional, quiet, yet trustful capitulation before the incomprehensibility of one's own existence, and thus also before God's incomprehensibility.... I believe that in life taken as a whole and at some particular specially blessed moments a decision is reached about one's own life.... One gives up everything, one lets everything go. And precisely in this seemingly dumb, dreadful and frightening emptiness there dawns the arrival of the infinite God of eternal life."[12]

Thus, *real* theological death may occur before medical death. It occurs through what Rahner and other theologians have called a "fundamental option," or a "freedom-decision."[13] Through this fundamental act of freedom a person decides with his or her being what and who he or she will *be* for all eternity. Death in the sense of this freedom-decision belongs intrinsically to the human person as a historical being.

No person can escape death and its seemingly destructive power. "All human beings," Rahner says, "die in such a way that everything is taken away from them, and Christians are convinced, while they live and when they die, that the ensuing emptiness is filled to the brim by what we call God. And basically we understand God — as the incomprehensible, of course — only when we say: He is the one who belongs in this ultimate existential void created by our death, as our fulfillment; as the fulfillment that is definitive; as the fulfillment that, as incomprehensible, we hope is our blessed salvation. We know very little about the beyond. We have in this respect become more discreet than former times, which painted grandiose pictures of the beyond.... To face death skeptically is not yet a denial of Christianity. Rather, human life has to pass through this apparent nullity, if it is to be fulfilled not by this or that, but by God."[14]

Purgatory

When most people die, they are still sinful and imperfect; yet, they do not deserve to be dammed. Given this anomaly, the Christian tradition has long taught the doctrine of purgatory, or a place of purification. Christian art and popular preaching often depict purgatory as a short-term hell. In this fiery anteroom to heaven a person suffers the penalties imposed by a vindictive God both for unrepented venial sins and repented, forgiven, but unexpiated sins.

Rahner distinguishes between the reality of purgatory and the images used to express this reality. When we sin by using our freedom against God, these free decisions become part of our being. Even our most interior sins embody themselves in our being. Even when we repent and confess our sins, these embodiments remain as inertia or resistance to loving God more deeply. Only prayer and penance remove these disordered embodiments.

As Rahner notes, "Of themselves these 'incarnations' remain and can in certain cases be changed, and work themselves off, only by a slow process in time which may last much longer than the free conversion in the person's center. The person, who has himself caused these 'exteriorizations' of his own guilt in his 'exterior' and his surroundings, inevitably experiences them as something causing him affliction, as a connatural punishment."[15] In Rahner's view, these embodiments of sin in our being cause experiential disharmony between ourselves, God, and others. In other words, the sinner creates his or her own purgatory. Sin, not God, punishes the sinner.

As unintegrated, sinful persons we create our own purgatory. The difference between what we should be and what we are creates purgatory. Do we truly love God totally and our neighbor as ourselves? A person, Rahner writes, "is perhaps sure that he loves God and yet does not venture to assert that he loves God with all his heart, that his whole existence is integrated into this love. He admits that in him are abysmal depths, a mass of instincts, a subconscious, an 'id,' etc., as realities of which it certainly cannot be said that they are all completely integrated into the personal decision of the subject that had decided or can decide finally for or against God.... Perhaps the unintegrated elements in man are incorporated into the final personal decision, now become definitive in death, in a lengthy 'process.' ... Why could not the 'duration' of the event of purification be identified with the diverse depth and intensity of the pain that man experiences in death itself, since there is a terrible difference between what he actually is and what he ought to be? Why should this pain (which is concretely identical with the individual character of dying proper to each person in accordance with his state) not itself be the purifying event which is supposed to constitute the essence of purgatory?"[16]

Thus Rahner understands purgatory as a purifying integration process that occurs in the act of dying. Every level of a person's being — many of which contain elements hostile to or alienated from God — now become painfully transformed into the person's freedom-decision to love God entirely. Because the person is actually dying into God's love, God's grace supports the person in the process by which he or she becomes totally in harmony with God.

This painful integration process is analogous to the pain a heavy smoker suffers after deciding from the depths of his freedom to quit this bad habit. The person soon experiences that he is not pure freedom. In the course of time the person will encounter distressing biological, physiological, and emotional resistance to his free decision to give up smoking. Perhaps even some of his smoking friends will intensify the suffering. On the other hand, supportive family and friends may help to lessen the person's pain.

By dying into God a person becomes more aware of his sinfulness, disorder, and disharmony. Rahner views this heightened awareness of self in the loving encounter with God as purgatory. Is not purgatory an encounter through death of the sinful, immature person with the all-holy God? This encounter with the all-holy God is of itself deeply humiliating, painful, and thus purifying. Purgatory *is* God's love purifying, enlightening, liberating, freeing, and thus bringing the person to perfection.

Hell

Rahner takes the Church's teaching on hell with absolute seriousness. He refuses to cast the topic aside in an embarrassed silence. On the other hand, he cautions about reading biblical depictions of the last things as if they were advance coverage or "previews of coming events." "What we know about Christian eschatology," he writes, "is what we know about man's *present* situation in the history of salvation. We do not project something from the future into the present, but rather in man's experience of himself and of God in grace and in Christ we project our Christian present into the future."[17]

Thus, biblical statements reveal only our present state before God — in this case, the *possibility* of eternal damnation. "The Christian," Rahner says, "will hope for death as eternal fulfillment but, at the same time, humbly fear the possibility that his or her end could really be one of loss."[18] Every Christian must say to self: "I *can* be lost and only through my own freedom."[19] In other words, Christian faith teaches that it is possible to be damned. However Rahner believes that through the misuse of our freedom *we* create hell — not God. The gates of hell are *freely* locked from the *inside*.

If one denies the possibility of hell, then one trivializes the biblical insight into the profound nature of human freedom, the seriousness of human history, and the radical nature of one's relationship with God. Human beings have the freedom to say "no" definitively and irrevocably to the God of love. Yet freedom to be definitively against God is the sheerest absurdity imaginable. "This 'no' in one's freedom," Rahner states, "is one of freedom's possibilities, but this possibility of freedom is always at the same time something abortive, something which miscarries and fails, something which is self-destructive and self-contradictory.... For every 'no' always derives its life from a 'yes' because the 'no' always becomes intelligible only in the light of the 'yes,' and not vice versa.... But we have to allow for such a real impossibility and self-contradiction in this 'no': the contradiction, namely, that this 'no' really closes itself and says 'no' to [God]...but at the same time lives by a 'yes' to this God."[20]

The analogies which follow might shed some light on what

Rahner means. Consider a person who says that there is no truth. There is a contradiction between what the person says and what the statement affirms: something true. The statement is self-contradictory. The "no" to truth in fact affirms it. The "no" lives by way of a "yes."

Consider a teenager who takes his parents to court to divorce them — an event that has already occurred a few times in the United States. By suing his parents for divorce, the teenager actually affirms them as his parents, regardless of the legal outcome. Once again we see a self-contradictory "no" living by way of a "yes."

Rahner considers a "no" to God as self-contradictory and as living from an even deeper "yes" because God created us, keeps us in existence, is the source of our freedom, and loves us — always and forever. We come from God and are meant for God. Human existence is not neutral. Engraved in our very being is the immense longing for God which can never be destroyed.

In every act of freedom, moreover, the person affirms God as the source of his or her freedom. The possible irrevocable "no" to God with our whole being affirms God as the source of our freedom. The "no" lives by the "yes" that God is the source of our freedom.

God created us to share his life; he loves us; Christ died for us: these realities stamp the very roots of our being. The inner obduracy which characterizes the state of hell cannot obliterate these realities. Moreover, to say "no" to them — although possible — is much more difficult than to say "yes" with one's entire being.

God is self-communicating love. This self-communicating love establishes itself historically in Christ and the saints. In Rahner's view, therefore, hell *is* God's love, Christ's love, the saints' love — to those who try to reject it. The person's free "no" to *irrevocable* love creates hell. Hell is therefore metaphysical schizophrenia; it is to be loved eternally by God, Christ, and the saints *and* to attempt eternally to escape from this love.

Rahner believes that one of the great achievements of the Second Vatican Council is its optimism about salvation. It is one of the ironies of history that from the beginning of Christianity right down to our century, a key question was: who will be saved? Since the Second Vatican Council the question is: will anyone be damned?

Rahner maintains that one may *hope* hell is empty. "I do not say," he writes, "that I could state in the form of an apodictic judgment coming out of my own self-understanding or out of a certain concept of God that 'hell' may be empty. One can hope, however, that radically forgiving love can ultimately bring it about that all human beings say a final yes to God so that actually no person must be damned in the face of divine judgment. So I may hope."[21] To him, a Christian must believe that the omnipotent God wills the salvation of all, that Christ died for all, that a free rejection of God is possible, and that one may hope that hell is empty. More than that Rahner will not say.

Bodily Resurrection

Rahner emphasizes that belief in bodily resurrection and eternal life with God as the fruit of his grace and of our history of freedom is an inalienable Christian faith-conviction. It must not be surrendered no matter how difficult it is for a contemporary person to believe it. Why live morally or seriously if life simply ends in a meaningless emptiness?

Rahner understands bodily resurrection as the definitive fulfillment of all aspects of the human person. Modeled after Jesus' resurrection, the person's resurrection is his or her lasting validity and permanence before God. In and through death God brings the entire human person to perfection.

Rejecting the somewhat Platonic traditional notion of a "separated soul," Rahner contends that through death the soul becomes even more deeply related to this one world — it becomes pancosmic. The soul does not, therefore, go somewhere to wait until the end of the world to be given back its body.

It is true, of course, that human perfection is attained only when God brings his one creation to completion at the end of the world. Nonetheless, "that does not mean," Rahner writes, "that the resurrection of the flesh cannot be seen as a process *beginning with death*."[22] To him, "the death of a person who really believes *is* a true dying-with Christ. It is the absolute triumph of life because his and our death *is a dying into resurrection*."[23] Thus, Rahner understands resurrection as occurring immediately through death, not at the end of the world.

The body, to Rahner, is not a thing but the soul's "expression of itself."[24] In a real way the world *is* to some extent the soul's expression in space and time. Moreover, the body is an ever-changing mystery not composed of a discrete number of particles. If one looks at a zygote, then the developing fetus, the growing baby, the developing child, the pubescent teenager, the young adult, the mature adult, and the very old person, one can rightly ask the question: "What *is* the human body? Whence its source of identity?"

Rahner certainly agrees with St. Paul that the physical body is not the spiritual body, that a person's corpse is not his or her body. Resurrection is not resuscitation. In fact no serious contemporary theologian need maintain "that the identity of the glorified body and the earthly body is only ensured if some material fragment of the earthly body is found again in the glorified body. For this kind of identity cannot even be found in the earthly body, because of its radical metabolic processes."[25] Thus, Rahner avers that "no one is in danger of defending a heresy if he maintains the view that the single and total perfecting of man in 'body' and 'soul' takes place *immediately after death....* So why should we not put the resurrection at that particular moment when the person's history of freedom is finally consummated, which is to say at his death?"[26] In a mysterious but real way, bodily resurrection as the person's total transformation takes place immediately in and through death.

Social Resurrection

We have already seen on numerous occasions that Rahner views the human person as both an individual and a social being. He speaks also of the one human race and of the solidarity that exists among all past, present, and future persons. If bodily resurrection fulfills the person, then the social dimension of the person must also be perfected.

The person dies to self into God but is given back to self as the full person he or she is, that is, as both an individual and a social person. The person dies not only into God but also into all other persons. Rahner says that "when a person loses himself in his unconditional surrender to the incomprehensible mystery of God, which appears like an ineffable darkness, then precisely at that moment he must be aware of himself as the one who vanishes; he must know whom he is surrendering in total abandonment to the eternal mystery. In this way he must be aware of *himself* in this final religious act in a quite unique way. But then, however, in this act he is not aware of himself as an individual and solitary subject, but as a person whose self is in solidarity with other persons, whose self communicates in selfless love with all other persons — *this* person surrenders himself to the eternal God. Thus he participates in that final act in which the Son surrendered his kingdom to the Father, and precisely by doing this entered into possession of his definitive and perfected relationship to the Father. In this final religious act the individual person dies into God not as an individual but, so to speak, as the whole of humanity with which every person is forever in solidarity. And precisely this act of the death of each individual and of the whole of humanity together is the true resurrection of every individual and of humanity together. All this takes place in Jesus, the one who passed through death, and only thus the risen one."[27]

Thus, a person dies and rises not only as an individual but in a true sense as the whole of humanity. To Rahner, not to believe in the social aspect of bodily resurrection is to betray the past, present, and future victims of atrocities. "If I were to ask," Rahner says, "how you relate to the dead of Auschwitz and Majdanek, and so forth, do you have the right and the courage to view these people simply as the fertilizer for a be-lated future, or must you give an account of yourself before them?"[28] In short, we die into God and into each other; we rise into God and into each other. Rahner views this as the basis of the Church's teaching on the "Communion of Saints" — the one history of human solidarity.

Resurrection of the World

Rahner views the human person as spirit-in-*world*. The human person is therefore individual, social, and worldly. If bodily res-urrection fulfills the person, then his or her worldly dimension must also be perfected. One dies not only into God, but also into the world. One rises not only in God but also as a transformed piece of this world. Through a person's resurrection, the resurrection of the world takes place.

Rahner unequivocally speaks of the "relationship between the fulfillment of an individual person through death, a fulfillment which is going on now continually, and the fulfillment of the human race and with it the *fulfillment of the world*, the world which has no other meaning to begin with except to be the realm of spiritual and personal history. But it also follows from the same principles that we cannot forgo a collective eschatology of the human race and of the *world* in favor of a purely existential interpretation of the individual eschatology of each individual. The fulfillment of the whole history of the human race is being accomplished in these individuals. After individuals have played their role here, they do not depart from a drama which as a whole continues on endlessly, a drama which continues to give spiritual individuals the possibility of performing their act on a stage which has been erected permanently. The *whole* is a drama, and the stage itself is also part of it. It is a dialogue between spiritual and divinized creatures and God, a dialogue and a drama which has already reached its irreversible climax in Christ. The world, then, is not merely a stopping-off place which is always there."[29]

Existentialists tend to understand resurrection either as an individual's coming to faith or as an individual's bodily resurrection. In contrast, Rahner emphasizes an individual bodily resurrection, the resurrection of the entire human race, and the resurrection of the *transformed* world. One might say with Rahner: through death into God, *I* shall rise bodily, *we* shall rise bodily, and the *world* will rise *transformed*.

In other words, just as the individual is transformed through death into bodily resurrection, so too are community — the communion of saints — and the entire cosmos so transformed. The world not only ends at some point, but it will also be transformed. God creates to communicate self to the individual, to the one human race, and to his one creation so that Christ may be all in all (Col. 3:11).

Heaven

Rahner does not understand heaven as a place existing out-side of time "at" or "in" which one arrives but as a metaphor denoting the fullness of salvation, the definitive perfection of the individual, bodily, social, and worldly person as spirit-in-world. It is a metaphor for the perfection of the God-creation relationship.

Heaven, to Rahner, is still growing because absolute fulfillment occurs only when God brings everything to fulfillment: the body-person, the one human race, and the history of the world. He also contends that in some sense we co-create heaven with God and eventually bring it to completion. To be sure, we, the one human race, and the world are saved by grace alone. Nonetheless, the person we become for all eternity is conditioned by what we have done and become in history.

We are not here, therefore, to weave baskets by day and undo them by night — in the style of some of the ancient monks. To Rahner's mind, "the inner-worldly task of individuals, of peoples, of nations, of historical epochs"[30] does indeed have a relationship to heaven, to God as the absolute future. What we do here has eternal significance. The striving for an inner-worldly utopia is definitely linked to completing heaven and to bringing about the end of the world — which only God can end.

Rahner stresses that "there exists between this inner-worldly utopia (taking 'utopia' in this context in a very positive sense) and Christian eschatology the same relationship of the unity and difference which, for example, a Christian sees in the light of the New Testament with regard to the unity and difference between love of God and love of neighbor.... By the very fact that a person performs his inner-worldly tasks out of love for others, there takes place for him the miracle of the love and of the self-communication in which God gives himself to man. There is, therefore, between inner-worldly utopia and eschatology the same unity and difference which is found in the ultimate and basic axiom of Christology: in Christology man and God are not the same, but neither are they ever separate."[31] In short, our earthly deeds contribute to a process only God can complete: bringing about the end of the world and perfecting heaven. Our task and God's task are not the same, but neither are they ever separate.

Heaven, to Rahner, has a Christological structure. Heaven is the perfection of the God-creation relationship begun in Jesus Christ, the God-Man. Rahner says: "This abiding of personal creatures in the presence of God essentially means the gathering of mankind into the definitive Body of Christ, into the 'whole Christ,' to commune with God who was made and remains *man;* hence it is that we shall 'see one another again,' that the human relationships of this world continue in heaven. This union of man with God and with his fellows means no loss or absorption of individuality; rather the closer man approaches to God the more his individuality is liberated and fortified."[32] One should also say that the more deeply a person enters into God's life, the more deeply he or she enters into the life of other human beings and into God's one creation.

The consummation of all things has been called the *parousia*, Christ's Second Coming, the resurrection of the flesh, and the Last Judgment. Rahner says it is also called the Judgment of *God*[33] because the completion of all things depends not on some independent evolutionary process but upon God's free initiative. It is also called the Judgment of *Christ* because of the Christocentric nature of all reality. It is also called *general* Judgment because everything — both good and evil — is completed. It is also called the *Last* Judgment because it is the final fulfillment which terminates history.

Rahner does not understand the Last Judgment in a juridical or extrinsic sense, a sort of great trial in the sky. "The experience of Jesus Christ's resurrection," Rahner affirms, "was precisely the beginning — not the interruption — of that single process which began at that time, has become irreversible and now goes on in the saving history of individuals and nations . . . drawing the world into God's transforming self-communication, the triumph of saving grace, or the final rejection of God's gift of himself whereby man pronounces his own judgment."[34] The Last Judgment is the full revelation of God's great love for everything he has created and the person's "yes" or "no" to this love.

Rahner maintains that despite everything we know from Scripture and the Christian tradition about afterlife, we still know very little. We must ponder these mysteries, but more importantly we must die daily and *worship* God. "In everything which man is and lives," Rahner says, "he passes through the zero point of death, and for Christian anthropology the God who alone is supposed to be man's absolute future remains the incomprehensible mystery to be worshipped in silence.... Consequently, as Christians we do not have to act as though we knew all about ourselves in heaven....But in reality this absolute fulfillment remains a mystery which we have to worship in silence by moving beyond all images into the ineffable."[35]

Christian Optimism

I know of no better way to end this chapter and book than with one of my favorite quotations from an interview given shortly before Rahner's death. When asked how he viewed the future of the world, of the Church, and of his own life, Rahner replied: "Let me begin with my own future. It comes down more or less to the hope for a few more years of 'noble peace,' as it is called in a Protestant hymn. This hope can prove false. And then beyond all earthly possibilities, hopes, and the like, I hope — with a bit of fear and trembling — for the absolute future, God himself. I would say that I hope for eternal life which transcends every humanly possible and attainable material, biological, and even spiritual achievement.

"Even if I cannot actually imagine what eternal life will really be like, I still have this hope. But from Christianity's good news in Jesus Christ I know that the absolute, everlasting, holy, eternally good God has promised himself to me as my future. I therefore have a solid, unconditional hope which, of course, is still subject to temptation as long as I am here on earth and have bad experiences in my life, in my community, in my country, and so on. That is self-evident. But till death's door I'll hold with a grip of steel — if I may say so — to the belief that there is an eternal light that will illumine me.

"And the same holds true for the earthly future of my own people or the world as a whole. I'm all for the courageous struggle for a better economic and social future. Given that one will stand accountable for one's obligations to society before God's judgment seat, I believe firmly that a person who is really convinced of this cannot and must not be outdone in this earthly task by those who do not believe in God, the absolute future.

"I would say that it would indeed be terrible and horrible if the world were to be destroyed by nuclear weapons or were to slip into ever-deepening economic misery. And everyone is obliged before God's eternal judgment to do everything one can to prevent such things from occurring. One will be held accountable for this. But if humanity or a nation were to fall into the abyss, even then I would still be of the unflinching conviction — and I hope to keep this conviction — that even such an abyss ultimately always ends in the arms of an eternally good, eternally powerful God."[36]

Notes

1. See "The Challenge of Growing Old," *The Content of Faith*, 129–31.

2. *Karl Rahner — I Remember*, 102.

3. For the sources of the remarks which follow, see *Karl Rahner — I Remember*, 101–6; *Karl Rahner in Dialogue*, 241–47.

4. *Karl Rahner — I Remember*, 103.

5. "The Challenge of Growing Old," *The Content of Faith*, 130.

6. *Karl Rahner in Dialogue*, 275.

7. Ibid., 209–10. Also see *Faith in a Wintry Season*, 103–4; *Karl Rahner — I Remember*, 105.

8. See *Karl Rahner in Dialogue*, 114–16.

9. *Faith in a Wintry Season*, 105 and 166; *Karl Rahner in Dialogue*, 246.

10. *Prayers for a Lifetime*, 19–20.

11. *Karl Rahner in Dialogue*, 245.

12. Ibid., 246. My emphasis.

13. Ibid., 86–87.

14. Ibid., 247.

15. "Remarks on the Theology of Indulgences," *TI II*, 197.

16. "Purgatory," *TI XIX*, 184–86.

17. *Foundations of Christian Faith*, 432.

18. *Karl Rahner in Dialogue*, 239

19. *Our Christian Faith*, 119.

20. *Foundations of Christian Faith*, 102.

21. *Faith in a Wintry Season*, 114. Also see *Karl Rahner in Dialogue*, 194–95.

22. "Resurrection of the Flesh," *Dictionary of Theology*, 444. My emphasis.

23. *Karl Rahner in Dialogue*, 246. My emphasis.

24. For the source of the remarks which follow, see "The Intermediate State," *TI XVII*, 114–24.

25. "The Intermediate State," *TI XVII*, 120.

26. Ibid., 115 and 120. My emphasis.

27. *The Courage to Pray*, 82. Translation emended.

28. *Karl Rahner in Dialogue*, 115.

29. *Foundations of Christian Faith*, 446. My emphasis.

30. Ibid., 446.

31. Ibid., 447.

32. "Heaven," *Dictionary of Theology*, 204.

33. For the source of the remarks which follow, see "Judgment, Last," *Dictionary of Theology*, 257–59.

34. "Parousia," *Dictionary of Theology*, 362.

35. *Foundations of Christian Faith*, 434.

36. *Karl Rahner — I Remember*, 110–11. Translation emended.